S·H·P
THE
SCHOOLS
HISTORY
PROJECT

Park

CASTLES & CATHEDRALS

Steve Buxton, Tim Copeland
and Colin Shephard
(Director, SHP)

Tim Copeland.

JOHN MURRAY

Acknowledgements

Illustrations by: Peter Bull; Jon Davies/Linden Artists; Steve Smith; Clive Spong/Linden Artists; Malcolm Stokes/Linden Artists; John Townson/Creation; Brian Watson/Linden Artists.

The authors and publishers would like to thank the following for permission to reproduce copyright photographs:

Cover *top* Christopher Nicholson/Robert Harding Picture Library; *right and left* Michael Holford; *bottom* Robert Harding Picture Library. **p.4** *top right* Cadw: Welsh Historic Monuments. Crown copyright; *centre left* English Heritage; *centre and centre right* Michael Jenner; *bottom left* Woodmansterne/Aerofilms; *bottom centre* Rheinisches Landesmuseum Trier; *bottom right* Woodmansterne. **p.5** *left* Colorsport; *right* Rheinisches Landesmuseum Trier. **p.6** English Heritage. **p.7** Cadw: Welsh Historic Monuments. Crown copyright. **p.8** Michael Holford. **p.10** Michael Holford. **p.11** English Heritage. **p.13** Ancient Art and Architecture Collection. **p.14** Worthing Museum and Art Gallery/Mark Sorrell. **p.16** Michael Holford. **p.18** Richard Shorter/Friends of Winchester Cathedral. **p.24** *top* Michael Holford; *bottom* British Library Add ms 15268 f.101b. **p.25** Walters Art Gallery, Baltimore. **p.27** English Heritage. **p.28** Aerofilms. **p.29** English Heritage. **p.32** *all* Mary Evans Picture Library. **p.33** *top* Woodmansterne; *centre* Robert Harding Picture Library; *bottom* English Heritage. **p.36** *all* Sonia Halliday and Laura Lushington. **p.37** by kind permission of the Dean and Chapter of Hereford. **p.38** Bodleian Library ms 288 f4v. by permission of the Warden and Fellows of New College, Oxford. **p.40** British Library Add ms 18850 f17v/Robert Harding Picture Library. **p.41** the Board of Trinity College Dublin. **p.42** Bibliotheque Royale Albert 1 er, Brussels. **p.44** *top left* Bridgeman Art Library; *top right* British Library; *bottom* Bridgeman Art Library/British Library. **p.45** *top left and centre right* Osterreichische Nationalbibliotek; *others* British Library **p.48** *top left* Michael Jenner; *top right* Graham Townson; *bottom left and right* Sonia Halliday Photographs; **pp.50–51** *all* from *Cathedral* by David Macaulay/HarperCollins Publishers. **p.52** *top* Sussex Archaeological Society. **p.53** Aerofilms. **pp.54–55** *all* Jim Belben. **p.56** *left* Woodmansterne; *right* Jim Belben. **p.57** *left* Woodmansterne; *right* Jim Belben. **p.58** Michael Holford. **p.60** *top right* English Heritage; *left* Jim Belben; *bottom right* Michael Holford. **p.61** Alan Sorrell/English Heritage. **p.62** *left* English Heritage; *right* Michael Jenner. **p.63** Jim Belben. **p.64** Rochester upon Medway City Council: section of a mural by Mr John Drummond FSIAD Hon Des RCA.

© Steve Buxton, Tim Copeland and Colin Shephard, 1992

First published 1992
by John Murray (Publishers) Ltd
50 Albemarle Street, London W1X 4BD

Typeset by Wearset, Boldon, Tyne and Wear
Printed in Great Britain by Cambus Litho, East Kilbride

A CIP catalogue record for this book is available from the British Library

Pupils' Book ISBN 0–7195–4952–3
Teacher's Evaluation Pack (Pupils' Book with 36pp teacher's notes) ISBN 0–7195–4979–5

THE SCHOOLS HISTORY PROJECT

This project was set up by the Schools Council in 1972. Its main aim was to suggest suitable objectives for History teachers, and to promote the use of appropriate materials and teaching methods for their realisation. This involved a reconsideration of the nature of History and its relevance in secondary schools, the design of a syllabus framework which shows the uses of History in the education of adolescents, and the setting up of appropriate examinations.

Since 1978 the project has been based at Trinity and All Saints' College, Leeds, where it is one of three curriculum development projects run and supported by the Centre for History Education. The project is now self funding and with the advent of the National Curriculum it has expanded its publications to provide courses throughout the Key Stages for pupils aged 5–16. The project provides INSET for all aspects of National Curriculum History.

ontents

Section 1   What are castles and cathedrals?   4

Section 2   The Norman Conquest   6

Were there castles in England before the Norman Conquest?   6

Why did William build castles?   8

Why did William want to control the Church?   16

Section 3   Castles and cathedrals in the Middle Ages   20

Life in the castle   20

Why did castle defences change?   24

Why did castles decline?   30

Points of view   32

Life in the cathedral   34

Section 4   How were castles and cathedrals built?   40

Section 5   Investigating a castle and a cathedral   52

Investigating Rochester Cathedral   54

The great pulpitum divide   58

Investigating Rochester Castle   60

Glossary   64

N.B. Words in SMALL CAPITALS are defined in the glossary on page 64.

What are castles and cathedrals?

1. Write a sentence explaining what you think a castle is. Write a sentence explaining what you think a cathedral is.
2. Look at these two definitions:
   - 'A place where people fight.'
   - 'A place where people worship.'

   Are these something like what you came up with? How good do you think these definitions are?
3. Look at the photographs in Sources 1–8. For each one decide whether it is a picture of a castle or a cathedral or neither. Note down reasons for your decision.

SOURCE 1

SOURCE 2

SOURCE 3

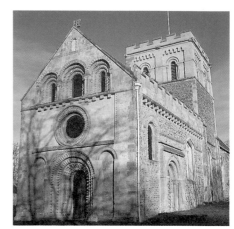

SOURCE 4

▲ **SOURCE 5**

▶ **SOURCE 6**

SOURCE 7

SOURCE 8

Captions

A The Great Hall of Conwy Castle in the 1280s

B Anfield football stadium, home of Liverpool F.C., built in 1920

C Lincoln Cathedral, built between 1200 and 1250

D Liverpool Catholic Cathedral, built in the 1970s

E Stonehenge. A circle of large stones thought to be a place where ancient Britons worshipped the sun or the moon, built around 5000BC

F Bamburgh Castle in the north east of England, built in 1300

G The parish church of St Mary, Iffley, built in the twelfth century

H The Porta Nigra, a Roman fortress for soldiers guarding the gates of a city, built in AD100

---

4. Copy the captions in the box and match each one with one of the pictures in Sources 1–8. Write the number of the correct source by each caption.
5. Does this make you change your mind about any of your answers to question 3?
6. Now that you have looked at all these pictures, do you think 'a place where people worship' is a good definition of a cathedral? For example, are all places where people worship cathedrals?
7. Do you think that 'a place where people fight' is a good description of a castle? For example, is that all that people did in castles?
8. Now write down as many words or phrases as you can think of that describe a castle or a cathedral.
9. Now look again at your definitions of a castle and a cathedral. Do you want to change anything about them?

An unusual case

Look at Source 9. Is it a castle or a cathedral?

SOURCE 9

Now compare Source 9 with Source 6. They show the same building. The Porta Nigra (the Black Gate) was built by the Romans to defend Trier, in Germany. When it was no longer needed as a fortress, the people of Trier converted it into a church. Then in the last century people became curious about the old Roman building. Parts of the church were stripped away to reveal the Roman fortress.

---

1. Make two outline drawings – 'before' and 'after' – and label them to show how the Porta Nigra was converted from a fortress into a church.

The example of the Porta Nigra suggests that the fortress and the church might have a lot in common. In this unit we will be able to see whether this is true of castles and cathedrals as well. And you will be able to decide if your definitions need to have anything added to them.

Were there castles in England before the Norman Conquest?

LOOK at the following statement from a recent history book: 'Before the Norman Conquest there were no castles in England.' After studying the information on these two pages you should be able to say whether you agree or disagree with it.

When the Romans came to Britain in AD43 they found many of the CELTIC people living in enormous hill forts such as Maiden Castle (see Source 1), which were home for entire villages or towns. The Romans had to fight fiercely to capture them. They must have been impressed by their strength, because they then built many of their own fortresses inside these hill forts.

The Romans also built fortresses all over Britain, wherever the Roman army was needed to fight or control the Britons — for example, there was a fort every mile along the length of Hadrian's Wall (see Source 3).

The Romans also tried but failed to conquer Scotland. If they had succeeded they would have come across another form of British defence, the *broch* (see Source 2).

The Romans left behind them in Britain many strong town defences such as those in London. However, many Roman towns fell into decay in ANGLO-SAXON times. In the ninth century, during King Alfred's reign, the Anglo-Saxons built their own style of defended town all over western and southern England. This was known as a *burh* (see Source 4). It had earth ramparts and ditches for defence from attacks by the Danes who had settled in the northern and eastern parts of England. In the earldom of Wessex no village was more than twenty miles from a *burh*, so when Wessex was attacked the people could retreat to safety inside the nearest *burh*.

In the 1060s, across the sea in Normandy, the Normans were building castles out of stone. Each castle was the home of a single lord and his family and he would use the castle as a base from which to control the surrounding countryside.

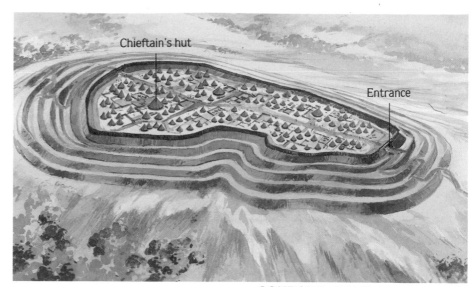

SOURCE 1 Artist's impression of Maiden Castle, a fortified Iron Age town used by Celtic people to defend themselves in the first century AD, before the Roman conquest of Britain

◀ **SOURCE 2** Reconstruction drawing of a *broch*. *Brochs* were built between 200BC and AD100. They are only found in north and west Scotland. A *broch* is like a heavily fortified house. It would be home for a single family or a group of families

SOURCE 3 Model of a milecastle on Hadrian's Wall, built in AD120 to house a small number of soldiers on sentry duty

▲ SOURCE 4 Reconstruction drawing of Wallingford burh, an Anglo-Saxon town defended by earth ramparts built in about AD900

1. Sources 1–4 show various ways in which people tried to defind themselves against attack in the 1200 years before the Norman Conquest of Britain. Draw a timeline from 200BC to AD1000 and mark on it when each of the types of defence shown were built.
2. Find similarities and differences between the different types of defence. Mention who lives there, who is being defended, and describe the defensive features.
3. Source 5 shows a Norman castle. In what ways is the Norman castle similar to the defences that came before it? In what ways is it different?
4. Do you agree with the statement at the top of the opposite page? Support your answer by referring to Sources 1–5 and the text.

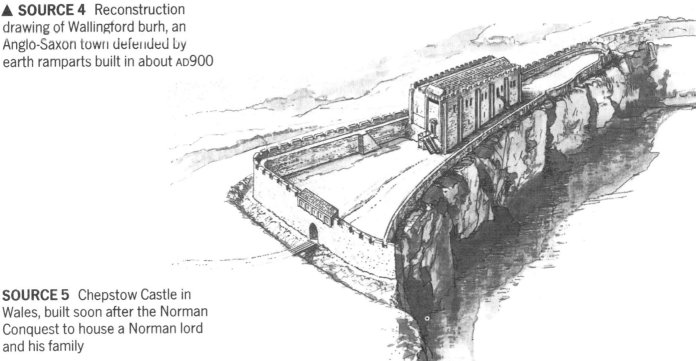

SOURCE 5 Chepstow Castle in Wales, built soon after the Norman Conquest to house a Norman lord and his family

Why did William build castles?

FROM your study of Medieval Realms you already know quite a bit about the Norman invasion of England in 1066 led by William, Duke of Normandy. In the next few pages we are going to investigate how the Normans used castles to conquer and control England.

Sources 1–4 all come from the Middle Ages and describe the Norman Conquest of England.

SOURCE 1 Written by William of Jumièges, a Norman monk

From Normandy, carried by the following wind, William crossed the sea and landed at Pevensey, where he at once built a strongly defended castle. Leaving a force of knights behind he hastened on to Hastings where he quickly raised another.

SOURCE 2 Written by Ordericus Vitalis, a monk who was half English and half Norman, in 1125

The fortresses which the Normans call castles had been very few in the English countryside and so the English, although they were brave and loved fighting, were too weak to withstand their enemies.

The King built a castle at Warwick and gave it to Henry Beaumont to guard. Next he built Nottingham castle and entrusted it to William Peverill. When the men of York heard this they were terrified and sent the King hostages and the keys of the city. As he was doubtful of their loyalty he strengthened a castle in the city and left trusted knights to guard it.

SOURCE 3 Numbers of houses the Normans demolished to build some of their first castles

Cambridge: 27
Gloucester: 16
Lincoln: 166
Norwich: 113

---

1. Choose two of Sources 1–4 which best show that William thought castles could help him conquer and control England. Give reasons for your choice.

SOURCE 4 Part of the Bayeux Tapestry showing the building of Hastings Castle – one of six Norman castles shown on the Tapestry

On the next seven pages we are going to investigate how castles helped William first to gain a secure foothold in England and then to get control of the whole country.

Stage 1:
A foothold in England

When they landed in England the Normans immediately built a castle within the walls of the massive old Roman fort at Pevensey. The next day they marched on to Hastings (leaving a few soldiers to guard Pevensey) and immediately built a second castle at Hastings, as shown in the Bayeux Tapestry (see Source 4).

It seems likely that parts of these two wooden castles – possibly the towers – were made in Normandy and carried over to England in sections by the invading army.

The Normans knew that, with a castle, a single lord and his few soldiers could control a wide area of land. So the first castles were simple and quick to build. The

Normans forced the English to build them, using wood and earth — readily available materials. Some medieval records suggest that these 'motte and bailey' castles could be built in about eight days.

After his victory at the Battle of Hastings William marched on Dover, where he built a third castle. On the map in Source 5 you can follow his progress as he marched on London, where he was crowned king ten weeks later.

In March 1067 William must have thought his grip on England was secure. He returned to Normandy to celebrate his victory and left his half-brother Odo of Bayeux in charge.

---

1. Do you think that William took the best route to London? Give your reasons.
2. Using the information in Source 5 make a list of castles built by William. Alongside each one show what it was guarding, e.g. a port, a road, a river.
3. On your own copy of Source 5 mark in the other places where you think William and his supporters should build castles. Give your reasons.

SOURCE 5 Map showing William's route to London and the first castles built by the Normans

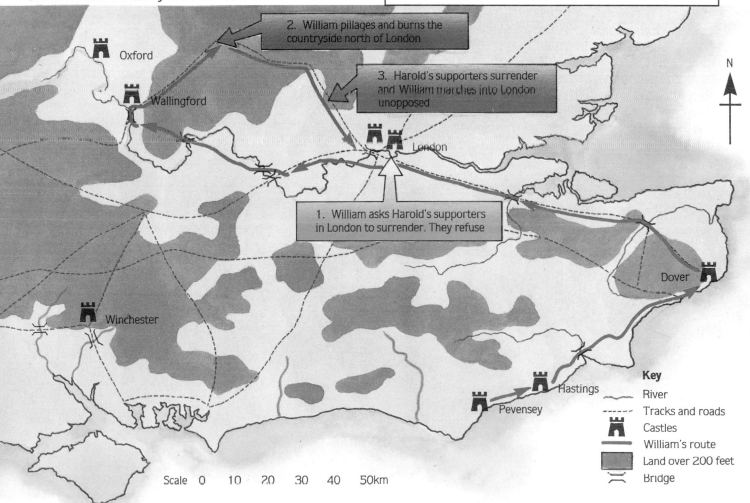

2. William pillages and burns the countryside north of London

3. Harold's supporters surrender and William marches into London unopposed

1. William asks Harold's supporters in London to surrender. They refuse

Oxford

Wallingford

London

Dover

Winchester

Hastings

Pevensey

N

Key
— River
----- Tracks and roads
Castles
— William's route
Land over 200 feet
Bridge

Scale 0 10 20 30 40 50km

WHY DID WILLIAM BUILD CASTLES?

What were the first Norman castles like?

Before we continue with the story of the Norman Conquest, we will see how historians have discovered what these first Norman MOTTE and BAILEY castles looked like. There is plenty of evidence to go on, but the sources we have do not always agree with one another. We have to compare the sources very carefully.

The only surviving written description of a motte and bailey castle was written by a French priest, Walter the Archdeacon, in his biography of John of Therouanne. In Source 6 he describes a castle John visited in northern France in about 1100.

SOURCE 7 The motte and bailey castle at Dinan, from the Bayeux Tapestry

Archaeologists have excavated a large number of sites of motte and bailey castles. They have found no remains of the castle buildings, but they have found holes in the ground from which they have drawn reconstructions like the one in Source 8.

SOURCE 8 An archaeologist's reconstruction of the motte (the mound) at Abinger, Surrey, built by the Normans in about 1100

SOURCE 6 Description of a motte and bailey castle

❝*It is the custom of the nobles of the neighbourhood, who spend most of their time fighting and slaughtering their enemies, in order to be safer from their opponents and in order to overcome their equals and suppress their inferiors, to make a mound of earth as high as they can, and encircle it with a ditch as broad and as deep as possible. They enclose the upper edge of this mount with, instead of a wall, a stockade of squared logs firmly fixed together, strengthened at intervals with towers, according to their means. Within this enclosure they build their house, a central tower which commands the whole place. The entrance may only be reached across a bridge, which springing from the outer edge of the ditch gradually rises, supported on pairs of pillars, or even triple pillars trussed together and suitably spaced, crossing the ditch with a gradual slope until it reaches the upper level of the mound at the level of the entrance gate to the stockade.*❞

---

1. Draw your own picture of the castle that Walter is describing in Source 6. Add labels to show:
   - the mound of earth
   - the central tower
   - the ditch
   - the bridge
   - the stockade and towers
   - the entrance.
   - the house

2. Make a list of differences between the motte and its buildings described in Source 6 and the reconstruction in Source 8. Which is most like the castle in the Bayeux Tapestry shown in Source 7?
3. Can you think of reasons for the differences between the description, the Tapestry picture and the reconstruction?
4. Which of the sources is most useful in helping us find out what a motte and bailey castle was like?
5. Why did archaeologists find no remains of the castle buildings in Source 8?
6. We know that the Normans were skilled at building in stone before 1066. What were the advantages and disadvantages of building the first castles in England out of wood and earth rather than stone?

SOURCE 9 Map showing all the sites of mottes that archaeologists and historians have discovered in England and Wales

Attached to the motte by a long stairway was a flatter area called the bailey. As you can see from Source 10 it too was surrounded by a ditch and palisade. The lord's soldiers, family and animals, as well as weapons and food supplies, would be housed in the bailey. One chronicle records that 3000 animals were grazed at the castle at Pickering. The lord's most valuable belongings could be rushed to the security of the motte if an attack came.

Although very simple in design the motte was very difficult to attack (see Source 11).

SOURCE 10 Reconstruction drawing of the motte and bailey castle at Pickering, Yorkshire, being built

SOURCE 11 Written by a modern historian in a book on castle sieges

66 *The attacker had to negotiate a ditch full of water or sharp spikes, storm up a slope too steep for horses, dismantle a palisade of stakes and thorns and finally capture a tower full of desperate men. In these circumstances his best ally would be fire.* 99

8. Using all the evidence on this page write a 'strengths and weaknesses' report on the motte and bailey castle.
   Write three paragraphs:
   ■ the strengths of the castle
   ■ the weaknesses of the castle
   ■ whether you think the motte and bailey castle was a success for the Normans.

7. Add to your drawing of the castle described in Source 6 the details of extra defences described by the writer of Source 11.

Stage 2:
Controlling the country

Early in 1068 King William returned from Normandy to find he had trouble on his hands. The city of Exeter was rebelling against Norman control.

William marched on Exeter. Ordericus Vitalis gives us a vivid picture of the defence of Exeter: William publicly blinding a hostage outside the city gates, the defenders baring their bottoms and farting at the Normans. Exeter withstood Norman attacks for eighteen days, before William accepted their surrender and (of course) built a castle to control the city.

But William's problems had only just begun. Throughout 1068 William was fully occupied putting down one rebellion after another – particularly in the Midlands and the North. To strengthen his position castles were built in Warwick, Nottingham and York. In Lincoln, Huntingdon and Cambridge castles were built to defend the main routes to the north.

Then, in 1069, William faced his greatest threat of all. In the north of England the English rebels had been promised the support of a large force of Danish soldiers. Foolishly, the Norman soldiers in York left their castle to attack the English rebels. They were slaughtered and their castle was destroyed. This was the signal for other rebels in the Midlands, the South West and the Welsh borders to join the rebellion and attack the hated Normans in their castles.

There were only about 7000 Norman knights to control more than a million English people. How could the Normans possibly control such a force? Source 12 suggests how their castles helped them.

Norman castles successfully withstood English attacks in Exeter, Montacute (Somerset) and Shrewsbury, and while the English rebels were occupied in these unsuccessful attacks William was able to pick off the rebel armies one by one.

When William finally removed the Danish threat by paying money to the Danish king he was free to put down the northern rebellion. He did so by destroying land, crops and villages with such ferocity that 100,000 English people died and whole villages were wiped out by the famine that followed. At the time of the Domesday Book fifteen years later vast areas of northern England were still wasteland.

By 1071 William's control of England was fairly secure and castles had been built throughout the country (see Source 13) by William or his barons and garrisoned with Norman soldiers.

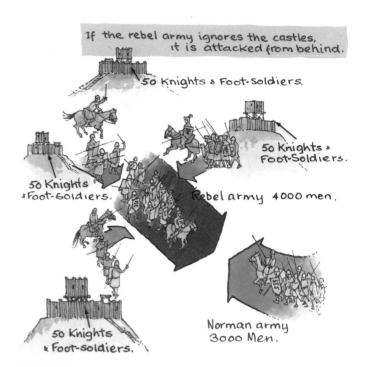

SOURCE 12 Diagram showing how a castle helped the Normans control the country

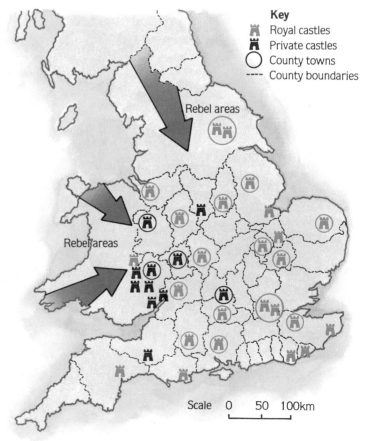

SOURCE 13 Castles built by William the Conqueror

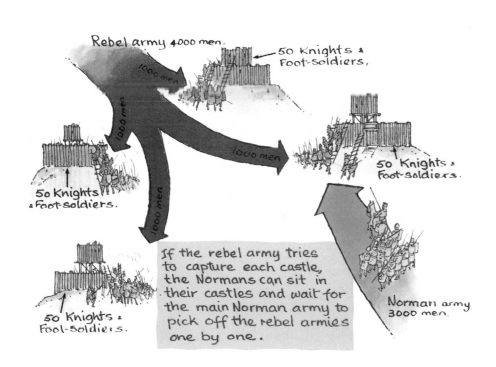

Rebel army 4000 men.

1000 men

1000 men

1000 men

1000 men

1000 men

50 Knights & Foot-soldiers.

50 Knights & Foot-soldiers.

50 Knights & Foot-soldiers.

50 Knights & Foot-soldiers.

Norman army 3000 men.

If the rebel army tries to capture each castle, the Normans can sit in their castles and wait for the main Norman army to pick off the rebel armies one by one.

The speedily built motte and bailey castle was ideal for the first stage of occupation of Britain, but to beat determined rebels William needed constantly to strengthen and improve his castles. As early as 1067 work was under way to rebuild the most important castles in stone. William brought Bishop Gundulf, one of his skilled builders, over from Normandy to rebuild London's most important castle, the Tower of London (see Source 14). Gundulf first built a stone curtain wall (the outer wall of the castle), then a square stone tower called the KEEP – the first and the biggest ever built in England, with walls nearly five metres thick at their base and about 30 metres high.

SOURCE 14 The keep at the Tower of London

1. Look at Source 13. You are William. It's important for you to rebuild your most important castles in stone. Which three castles would you rebuild in stone first?

13

Stage 3:
The Feudal System

As the Normans strengthened their grip on the conquered English, William divided up his new land.

> **SOURCE 15** Written by William of Poitiers, a Norman chronicler
>
> 66 *In his castles William placed loyal and able guards whom he had brought over from France, together with a large number of horses and foot-soldiers. He distributed the rich land among them, in return for which they willingly undertook hardships and dangers.* 99

Most of the land in England was carved up into less than 200 enormous estates, called honours, and distributed among the Norman lords. With the land came the people who lived there – English people who greatly resented their new Norman lords.

This system of holding land in return for loyalty and/or service was common in Europe and was called the Feudal System.

At the top were the Norman lords. At the bottom were the English and Welsh peasants. One of the first things the Norman lord did when he took over his new lands was to force his VILLEINS to build him a castle. To rub salt into their wounds the Normans even used an ancient English law – requiring everyone to do their bit in building the defences of a town – to justify their action.

Source 13 shows William's royal castles, but there really weren't very many of those. The vast majority of Norman castles were built by William's lords and were

SOURCE 16 How the Feudal System worked

Grants land to → Promises to provide Knights for the army for 40 days a year

Grants land to → Promises to serve in the army for 40 days a year

Grants land to → Promises services and payment to

guarded by the lords' personal armies. There can have been few things which proved the power of the Normans to the defeated English better than a new castle towering above the villages it controlled. It was in the castle hall that the local courts usually met. It was to the castle that a peasant went to pay taxes, to seek justice and to offer services. And just as William had improved his castles, so the BARONS improved theirs to provide even better protection for themselves, their families and their loyal soldiers against even the most determined attackers.

1. Look at Source 17. Can you see the original motte?
2. List three ways in which the baron has made Bramber castle stronger or more comfortable since the original motte and bailey was built.

SOURCE 17 A reconstruction drawing of Bramber Castle by Alan Sorrell

3. The English villeins must have had mixed feelings about the lord and his castle. Try to work out what some of these villeins might have been thinking shortly after the Normans had forced them to build a castle.

SOURCE 18 Plan of land around Chepstow

Key

▲ Settlements

---- Boundary of lordship of Chepstow in 1100

→ Attacks from Welsh

Woodland

Rivers and streams

Marsh

High ground

→ Attacks from other barons

Scale 0 — 10km

Activity

You are William Fitz Osbern, a Norman lord who has been granted land by King William I. Source 18 shows you a plan of your lands.

King William will not tell you to build your castle in a particular place, but he expects you to hold the lands for him, so the castle had better be on a suitable site. It must also protect you and your family.

Your first task is to decide where to build the castle. There are a number of points to consider:

■ You need a strong position, easy to defend, using the natural features of the land (e.g. rivers, high ground) to your advantage. Think about where attacks might come from.

■ You have to be in a position to control the people if they give you trouble, and you must be able to get to your lands easily to inspect them.

■ Where is your water and food going to come from?

■ Where will you get the building materials you need? Moving heavy materials takes time and is expensive.

■ Who will build the castle — where do your villeins live?

■ Do you want a moat around your castle? If so, how will you get the water to keep it filled up?

■ Would it impress the English more if you forced them to demolish a few of their homes to make room for the castle?

1. On the copy of Source 18 which your teacher will give you, mark a position for your castle and list the reasons why it is a good place.

2. You have just completed your castle. You are writing to King William, who wants a regular update on what his lords are doing. Explain to King William, using diagrams if necessary, where you have decided to build your castle and why it will help you keep a secure hold on the lands he has granted to you.

3. Write the King's reply to William Fitz Osbern, thanking him for his letter, giving your view of his plans and summarising how his castle fits into your overall plan for the role of castles in conquering and controlling England.

4. One chronicler called the Normans' castles 'the bones of the kingdom'. What do you think he meant by this?

Why did William want to control the Church?

The English Church in the 1060s

In 1060 England had been a Christian country for many centuries. The timeline shows how Christianity grew.

> **337** Christianity becomes the official religion of Roman Britain. By 400 Christian chapels are being built in Roman villas and towns.
>
> **450** England is invaded by the pagan ANGLO-SAXONS. Christianity almost disappears from England.
>
> **563** Monks from Ireland set up the first Christian monastery in Britain, Iona. In 635 they set up the monastery of Lindisfarne. Monks spread Christianity in northern England.
>
> **597** The POPE sends St Augustine to England to convert the Saxons. He builds churches at Canterbury and Rochester in Kent.
>
> **669** The Church is reorganised into areas called dioceses, each run by a bishop based in a cathedral.
>
> **974** Largest Saxon cathedral, Winchester, is completed.

By 1060, religion played a part in every aspect of people's lives. It was with them every minute of the day. People believed that God and the saints controlled their health, the weather, good fortune in business and everything else.

Everybody went to church on Sundays and holy days, and there were special services for the important stages of people's lives, such as birth, marriage and death.

Most people could not read the Bible for themselves or understand church services, which were in Latin. Instead, they learned about the life and teachings of Christ from the priests' sermons and the paintings which could be found on the walls of most churches.

People were desperate to keep out of Hell, where they would stay in agony for the rest of time. To get to Heaven people had to be free of sin. Since most people were committing sins all the time this was very difficult. They had to confess these sins to the priest and be genuinely sorry for committing them.

SOURCE 1 The Chaldon mural. The painting shows a ladder going from Earth, through Hell and finally reaching Heaven. The souls of dead men and women are trying to climb the ladder to get to Heaven

The priest was there to help the people live good lives and get to Heaven. A priest devoted his life to God and had special powers, like being able to forgive people's sins. He baptised babies and gave dying people the last rites to clean them from sin. He was one of the most important people in the village. The Church was the only organisation which had a representative in every single village.

Every village was part of an enormous DIOCESE centred on the cathedral. Normally, the villagers would not have much to do with the cathedral, which might be up to 100 miles away. But at PILGRIMAGE time many villagers would travel to the ancient Saxon cathedrals where the RELICS of the most holy English saints were kept.

All the churches and priests in the diocese were under the control of the bishop. He lived in a palace built alongside the cathedral. He was a powerful man. Not only was he the Pope's (and therefore God's) representative in the diocese, he was also an adviser to the king.

Pope, Head of Church.

Archbishops governed English Church.

Bishops governed each diocese.

Priests ran the church in each village.

The people give a tenth of their goods to the Church.

SOURCE 2 Who was who in the Church

Before he invaded England, William of Normandy sent messengers to the Pope asking him to bless the invasion. He promised to reform the English Church if he was successful. The Pope, who had been educated in Normandy, obliged, and so when William set sail for England he carried with him a battle flag which had been blessed by the Pope.

---

1. Here is a list of things happening in Hell. Match these up with the figures in the painting.
   - murderers being put into a pot of boiling water
   - a money lender burning on flames, still counting his gold
   - a bridge of spikes for dishonest tradesmen (can you see which tradesmen are shown?)
   - demons pulling people off the ladder
   - a woman having her hand bitten by a dog. She is confessing to pampering her own dogs with meat when poor people were going hungry
   - a drunken pilgrim drinking from a wine bottle.
2. Here is a list of things happening in Heaven. Match these up with the figures in the painting.
   - Christ defeating the Devil, who has his hands tied
   - St Michael weighing people's goodness to see if they should go to Heaven or Hell (what do you think the demon on the left is doing?)
   - angels helping people up the ladder.
3. How do you think you would have felt if you were a medieval peasant in church looking at this picture? Would you have been terrified, amused, worried or bored?

---

4. Here are a number of reasons why William might have wanted the Pope's blessing. Which do you think might be the most important? Give reasons for your answer.
   - William wanted God on his side to make sure he won.
   - William knew how powerful the Church was in England and wanted to make sure the Church did not resist his invasion.
   - The English earls were Christian – perhaps they might want to fight against William, but surely they wouldn't want to fight against God.

Activity
You are one of William's Norman barons. What arguments will you use to persuade him that it's important to get control of the Church as quickly as possible after conquering England?

After the Conquest

When William won the Battle of Hastings he immediately built a new monastery at the place which came to be called Battle. The altar was placed directly over the spot where Harold was killed. William also sent Harold's battle flag back to the Pope to show that he had won the battle.

Then he began the reorganisation of the Church that he had promised the Pope.

Key

△ Cathedral

---- Boundary of diocese

SOURCE 3 Map showing new cathedrals built by the Normans. Sometimes the Normans demolished the old English cathedral and built a new one on the same site, as at Winchester. They abandoned any Saxon cathedrals which were out in the country and built new ones in the important towns

SOURCE 4 From *The Norman Heritage* by Rowley, written in 1973

❝ In 1069, Stigund was removed as Archbishop of Canterbury and replaced by William's friend and confidant Lanfranc.

Lanfranc was a resourceful politician . . . a sincere churchman . . . and a reformer. He brought with him to England a group of pupils and colleagues from Normandy . . . including his nephew Paul, who became the Abbot of St Albans, Gundulf, who became Bishop of Rochester, and Crispin, Abbot of Westminster. Within ten years of the Conquest all the bishops except the Bishop of Worcester were Normans. ❞

SOURCE 5 Some incidents recorded by medieval chroniclers

❝ ■ At St Albans the new Norman abbot smashed up the graves of past abbots, calling them 'uncultured idiots'.

■ Saints worshipped by the English came in for similar treatment. At Evesham, Walter, the new Norman abbot, set fire to the relics of English saints saying that if they really were holy then the fire would not hurt them. Nobody recorded whether the relics survived. ❞

SOURCE 6 Written by an English monk in Durham in 1099

❝ The space between the church and the castle, which had been occupied with a number of poor houses, the bishop reduced to a bare field so that the church should be untouched by the contamination of filth or dangers of fire. ❞

SOURCE 7 Aerial view of Winchester Cathedral, which the Normans started to build in 1079. The orange line shows the position of the old Saxon cathedral, which had been the biggest in England before 1066. The Normans demolished it

SOURCE 8 From the English monk Eadmer's *History of Recent Events in England*, written not long after William's reign

William would not allow anyone in England, except with his permission, to accept any letter from the Pope in Rome, if it had not first been submitted to the King himself.

Also he would not let the Archbishop of Canterbury lay down any laws in the Church unless they were agreeable to the King's wishes.

Then again he would not allow any of his bishops, except on his instructions, to excommunicate one of his barons for incest or adultery, even when notoriously guilty.

SOURCE 9 From the Book of Ely, written by English monks

All that was finest of the art treasure was carried off to King William's treasury.

SOURCE 10 From the writings of the English monk William of Malmesbury (1132)

England has become a residence for foreigners and the property of aliens. At the present time there is no English earl, no bishop, nor abbot.

About the demolition of Worcester Cathedral in 1084

We poor wretches destroy the works of our forefathers that we may get praise for ourselves. That happy age of holy men knew not how to build stately churches; under any roof they gave themselves as 'living temples' to God and by their example encouraged those they cared for to do the same; but we alas try to build up stones and neglect the looking after people's souls.

Before 1066 there were less than 70 monasteries and nunneries in England. William immediately granted land to 30 Norman monasteries to set up branches in England.

1. Divide your page into four, and write these headings in the four boxes:
   - Church leaders
   - Church buildings
   - Land
   - English saints
   Using Sources 3–10, fill in as much detail as you can in each of the boxes about how William changed the English Church.
2. Which of Sources 3–10 are helpful in showing us what the English thought of the changes?
3. Do you think they show us what all the English people thought of the changes?
4. Which of the measures described in Sources 3–10 would have most effect on ordinary English people?
5. On your own copy of this cartoon, fill in the thought bubbles with what the English people might think about the actions of William and his bishops.
6. Do you agree or disagree with this statement? Explain your answer.
   - 'The Normans built fewer cathedrals than castles. This shows that their castles were more important than their cathedrals in conquering and controlling Britain.'

Life in the castle

1. Study Sources 1 and 2 very carefully. With a partner try to identify differences between the two pictures. Make a list of your findings.

2. Write a description of life in the castle in 1300. Emphasise in the description how the castle has changed since 1100.

   Make sure that your description includes the following details:
   - how comfortable it is to live in
   - how crowded it is
   - how much privacy the lord has
   - how clean and hygienic it is
   - how secure it is from attack
   - how easy it is to get food and water.

SOURCE 1 A castle in 1100

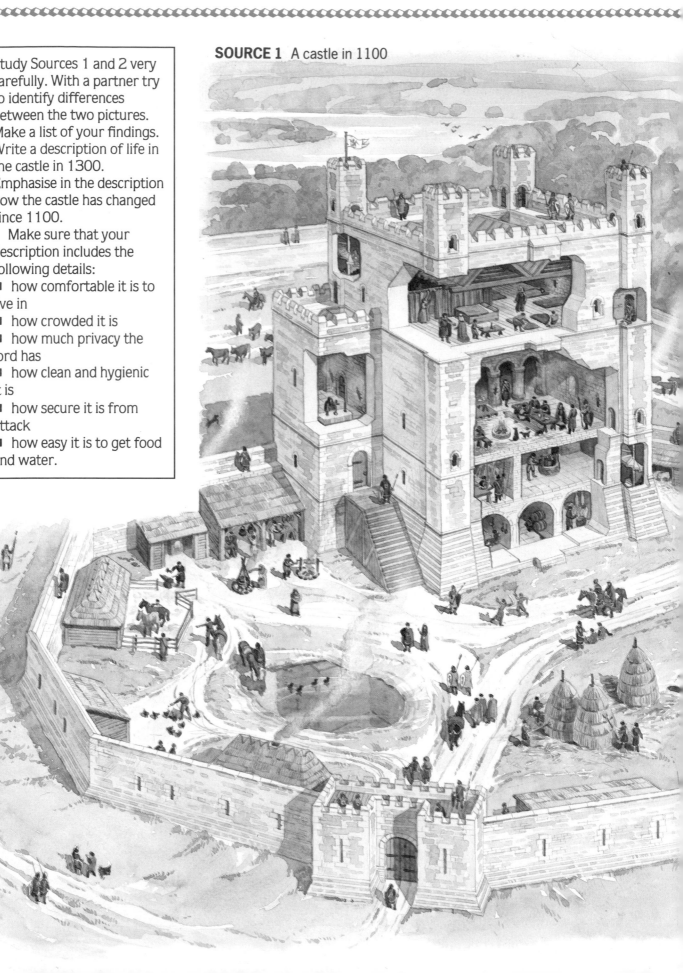

SOURCE 2 A castle in 1300

It's all too easy to make the mistake of thinking that medieval castles were constantly at war. In fact, a castle might have seen only two or three days' serious fighting in 200 years.

As you can see from Sources 1 and 2, the castle was a home. So there were children playing, adults working and people cooking, eating and drinking. Sometimes there were arguments and fights, but there would also be music and singing, or parties and special feasts, especially when an important visitor came to stay or at holiday times.

Many servants and officials were needed to keep the castle going — to look after the water supply, drains, privies, pits and sewers; to stock the drink store, the pantry (from the French word for bread, *pain*), the brewhouse and the bakehouse; to run the workshops, including blacksmiths' and carpenters' shops, and the armoury.

In some castles there were fishponds, vineyards and orchards to be tended, as well as the lord's animals — his horses, farm animals, doves, falcons and hunting dogs.

The castle was also a power base. In the most important room in the castle, the great hall, the lord or his officials held law courts, collected taxes and controlled the peasants' work on his farm land.

The castle was like today's law court, farmhouse and family home rolled into one.

LIFE IN THE CASTLE

What was a day in the castle like?

Sources 1 and 2 on the previous page are a bit of a cheat — not all the events shown would be happening at the same time. So let's look more closely at what it might be like in the castle at two different times of day.

SOURCE 3 The castle in the morning

SOURCE 4 The castle at dinner time

A visit from the king

In the Middle Ages the king was always on the move. He never stayed in one place for long. He could not just pick up a telephone to check how things were going in Chester or Gloucester, and he didn't always trust his advisers, so he had to visit troubled areas of his country to make sure people stayed loyal to him. Sometimes he stayed at his own castles, sometimes with his barons — which helped keep the expenses of the royal household down. As he moved from castle to castle, he travelled with a small army of servants, huntsmen, soldiers, barons and officials. With such a large retinue the king might only travel about 20 miles a day, and would sometimes stay in one place for only a night. You can imagine the work that would be involved in getting a castle ready for so many people for just one night.

Activity

Choose one of the following characters — blacksmith, cook, chaplain or lady — and use the information on pages 20–23 and your own imagination to write a diary entry for the day of the king's visit.

Think about how your character would dress, what he/she would have to do during the day, what he/she would think of the king's visit.

Why did castle defences change?

WHEN William the Conqueror's son King Henry I died in 1135, England was plunged into more than twenty years of civil war.

Henry had no heir. His son had been drowned in an accident at sea in 1120. His nephew Stephen took the throne, but was opposed by many English lords, who openly fought against the king and against each other. It was a dangerous time to be living in England.

Some estimates say that more than 1000 new, unlicensed (and therefore illegal) castles were built as 'robber barons' grabbed land from the king or from their neighbours and built castles to defend themselves.

King Henry II demolished most of these castles when order was restored after 1155, but 60 years later during the reign of King John the barons were once again at war with the king.

Events like these helped fuel a kind of medieval arms race. A medieval castle was usually at peace, but it had to be ready for war. At any time violence could erupt: any lord could become a warlord and his servants could become an army. As attackers thought up new methods of attacking castles, castle builders invented new means of defence or counter-attack. Each new castle that was built had some of the best and latest defensive features.

Methods of attack

1. Sources 1–3 come from the Middle Ages. They show attacks on castles and city walls. Study each one carefully and write a description of what the attackers are doing.

SOURCE 1

SOURCE 2

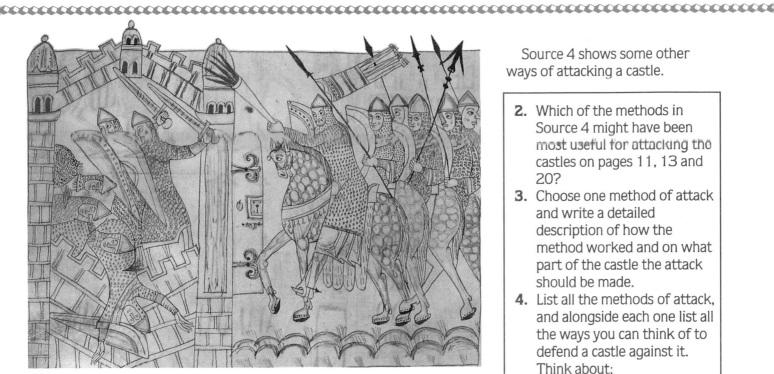

▲ SOURCE 3

Source 4 shows some other ways of attacking a castle.

2. Which of the methods in Source 4 might have been most useful for attacking the castles on pages 11, 13 and 20?
3. Choose one method of attack and write a detailed description of how the method worked and on what part of the castle the attack should be made.
4. List all the methods of attack, and alongside each one list all the ways you can think of to defend a castle against it. Think about:
   - the site — where you build your castle
   - improved defences
   - new building — or extending the building
   - new weapons or gadgets.

Trebuchet
(for throwing stones)

Crossbow

How to Attack a Castle

Siege tower

Scaling ladders

Mine

Fire

Battering ram

SOURCE 4 Methods of attacking a castle

WHY DID CASTLE DEFENCES CHANGE?

Methods of defence

Now compare your answers to question 4 on page 25 with some of the solutions devised by the castle builders.

Moats (1)

A moat prevented mining, because a MINE under the moat would flood. It also made it very difficult for attackers to use siege equipment such as scaling ladders or siege towers, although they could still fill the moat with stones and logs to allow their siege engines to get close to the wall.

Protection for the defenders (2)

Adding shutters in the CRENELLATIONS and making windows thinner made it more difficult for an attacker to shoot a defender.

Round towers (3)

A castle wall needed towers. They stuck out from the walls, so castle defenders could shoot at attackers who were at the bottom of the wall. But these had always been a very vulnerable part of castle defences. The square corners were easy to mine. Round towers were more difficult for defenders to mine, and more difficult to damage with stone throwers as the missiles just glanced off.

Bratticing (4) and machicolations (5)

Bratticing was a wooden platform which could be specially built when a siege was threatened. It allowed defenders to drop objects onto attackers or to fire at them from above.

Machicolations had the same purpose but were permanent and built into the walls of the castle.

Gatehouse

The gate was one of the most vulnerable parts of the castle. It needed defending in many different ways.

A barbican — an extended gatehouse outside the castle — might combine round towers, machicolations and thin windows, as well as a drawbridge, one or even two portcullises, and 'murder holes' inside the gateway in case any attackers got that far.

SOURCE 5 Castle defences

SOURCE 6 Gatehouse defences

Counter-attack

Counter-attack was an important form of defence. For example, castle defenders could use ingenious devices such as the 'crow' — an enormous fishing line which could swoop down and pick up an attacker, who was then kept as a hostage or tortured for information about the enemies' plans.

Then there was the counter-mine, where defenders dug under an attacker's MINE causing the tunnel to collapse before it could reach the wall and do damage.

1. *Either* draw your own picture of a 'crow', *or* draw a cross-section through a wall showing how a counter-mine would work.
2. Source 7 shows Warkworth Castle in Northumberland. Identify which of the defensive features described on this page have been included at Warkworth.
3. On the outline drawing of the ruined walls of Warkworth which your teacher will give you, draw what you think the walls and fortifications would have looked like.
4. If you were defending Warkworth, what would you do if the BAILEY was taken?
5. If you were attacking Warkworth, which side would you attack the castle from? What weapons would you use?

SOURCE 7 Warkworth Castle in Northumberland

Concentric castles

By the middle of the thirteenth century very few new castles were being built in England. It was a more peaceful place and they were no longer needed. But castle building continued on a grand scale in Wales. Between 1277 and 1295 King Edward I built ten strong new castles in Wales to keep his hold on each part of the coast and countryside as he conquered it (see Source 8).

Edward wanted the strongest castles money could buy. He had spent time as a young man fighting in the Crusades, and had seen at first hand the strength of the Crusader castles and the castles of Spain, France and Italy. So he brought in one of Europe's leading castle designers to be in charge of the work. This man was known as James of St George. James did not disappoint his new employer.

Source 9 shows one of Edward's castles, Beaumaris. It incorporated many of the new developments and improved them even more to make it almost impossible to attack the castle successfully.

Beaumaris is a CONCENTRIC CASTLE. It has no keep. Instead, there is a high inner wall and a lower outer wall. Beaumaris had no blindspots. Defenders could shoot at attackers from both walls and from towers at regular points along both walls.

Even if the attackers breached the first wall, the second inner wall was bigger and stronger. Siege engines could hardly be used. It is not difficult to see why Beaumaris was never attacked.

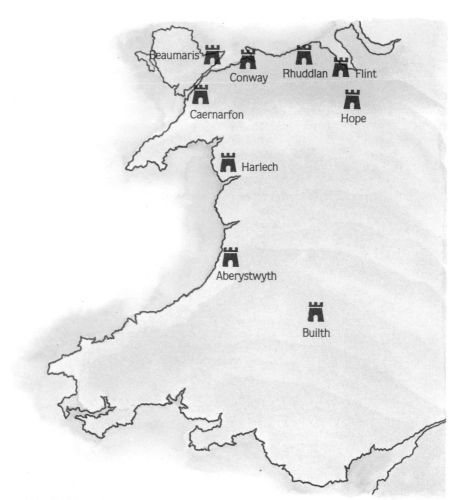

SOURCE 8 Map showing Welsh castles built by Edward I

SOURCE 9 Beaumaris Castle

1. Draw a simple plan of Beaumaris Castle and mark the following features: outer wall, inner wall, outer bailey and inner bailey.
2. Mark on your plan where you think the castle's occupants would live.

Gunpowder and castles

Although cannons and guns were first used in the early fourteenth century, it was another 200 years before they were really much use in warfare. To start with, gunpowder's main use was to frighten the enemy.

But as gunpowder became more effective it began to have an effect on the design of some new castles, such as Deal Castle, built in the sixteenth century by Henry VIII (Source 10).

1. How have the designers of the castle in Source 10 made their castle more able to use or withstand the use of gunpowder?

Activity

It is 1300. You have been employed by a rich and powerful lord to design a new castle for him on lands which he has just taken over. The existing castle is a simple square stone KEEP with a thin CURTAIN WALL running around it. You want to include in your designs some of the latest improvements in castle defence, as well as ensuring that the lord and his family are as comfortable as possible. However, you will have to sell your ideas to the lord as he will only agree to pay for them if he is convinced that they will work.

Prepare sketches that show the features you want to build into the design of your castle. Add notes to describe the features and the reasons why you think they should be included.

Then write a letter to go with your designs explaining how the new castle will be a change for the better for the lord and his family.

Walls 5m thick

Rounded walls deflect missiles

Low towers hidden from attackers by defensive walls

Ditch

Earth walls

Gunports

SOURCE 10 Deal Castle in Kent

Why did castles decline?

In 1534 a historian called John Leland began a tour around Britain. He wanted to catalogue all the old buildings in the country, but he went mad in 1550 and never completed the book he planned to write about them. He did, however, leave behind the notes that he made on his travels. He was particularly interested in castles. Source 1 gives extracts from his notes.

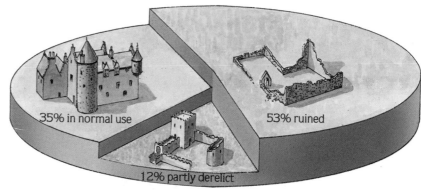

SOURCE 2

John Leland described more than 250 castles in his notes. Source 2 shows you the condition they were in.

35% in normal use

53% ruined

12% partly derelict

SOURCE 1 From John Leland's notes, 1534–43

❝*Brackley: there was a fair castle. The site and hill where it stood is yet evidently seen, but there is not seen any piece of wall standing.*

Elmley: there standeth now but one tower and that partly broken. As I went by I saw carts carrying stone away to mend Pershore Bridge, about eleven miles off.

Hedingham: the castle was in much ruin except the gatehouse and dungeon tower.

Fulbrook: Sir William Compton, seeing it go to ruin, took parts of it away to build his own house at Compton.

Haringworth: a right goodly manor place . . . built like a castle. The first court is clean down save the gatehouse. The inner part is well maintained.

Kenfig: in ruin and almost swallowed up by the sands the Severn Sea casts up.

Nottingham: much part of the west side of it is in ruins. The east side is strong and well towered, as is the south. But the most beautiful part for living is the north, where King Edward IV began a sumptuous piece of stonework.

Oystermouth: ruined remains of a castle destroyed by Prince Llywelyn.

Pickering: the castle wall and towers be well. The living quarters that be of timber be in ruin.

Richard's Castle: still stands but going to ruin. There is a poor timber house of a farmer inside the castle.

Sheriff Hutton: the castle was well maintained because the late Duke of Norfolk lay there ten years.

Trematon: the ruins now serve for a prison.

Warwick: magnificent and strong. King Richard III began to build a strong piece for guns on the north side of the castle.❞

---

1. Which castles mentioned in Source 1 were in ruins?
2. Which castles were in ruins but still being used in some way?
3. Which castles were partly ruined?
4. Which castles were in a good state of repair?
5. Which castles had been improved or repaired by the king?
6. What clues does Source 1 give us as to why some of the castles were ruined?

Clearly the castle was in decline by this time. On the border with Scotland, which was still occasionally at war with England, the castle was still an important means of defence. But in England many castles were simply being abandoned for more comfortable manor houses. The castle was no longer needed.

Historians sometimes blame the development of gunpowder for the castle's decline, but cannons and guns were not really effective in warfare until well after Leland's time. The main change brought about by gunpowder was that castle defences began to include gunports (holes in the walls through which guns could be fired at attackers). Gunpowder may explain why very few new castles were built in the late Middle Ages, but not why so many castles were abandoned. The reasons run much deeper than that.

Warfare had changed. In the early years of the Middle Ages a lord always had to be ready to defend himself against attack, but during the civil war known as the 'Wars of the Roses' (1455–1487) there was only one castle siege. All the important fighting was done by well equipped mobile armies out in the open field.

Society had changed as well. The lord was not as important as he had been in 1066. The government ran the country from London. As the king became more powerful he had less need of the local lord. The Feudal System was weakened as more villagers bought their freedom, and as townspeople became richer and more powerful and sent their own representatives to Parliament.

So, instead of castles, the lords built themselves fortified manor houses, which combined an element of defence with comfort and luxury.

7. Do the two castles in Sources 3 and 4 fit the general pattern described on this page?
8. Do you think Sir Roger's castle is well defended?
9. Do you think William Douglas' castle is likely to be as comfortable as Sir Roger's?
10. Why do you think two such different castles were being built in the same decade?

Activity

Split into groups. Each group should look through pages 20–31 for evidence of the factors that led to the changing design of castles. Find examples of:
■ political factors, e.g. a decision made by a king
■ social factors, e.g. society becoming more peaceful
■ technological factors, e.g. new inventions in defence.
Write each factor on a separate piece of card, and then try to put them in order of importance.

SOURCE 3 Herstmonceaux Castle in Sussex, rebuilt in the 1440s by Sir Roger Fienes, the King's Treasurer

SOURCE 4 Threave Castle on the Scottish borders, rebuilt in the 1440s by William Douglas, a Scottish lord who had led an attack on Warkworth Castle in Northumberland

Points of view

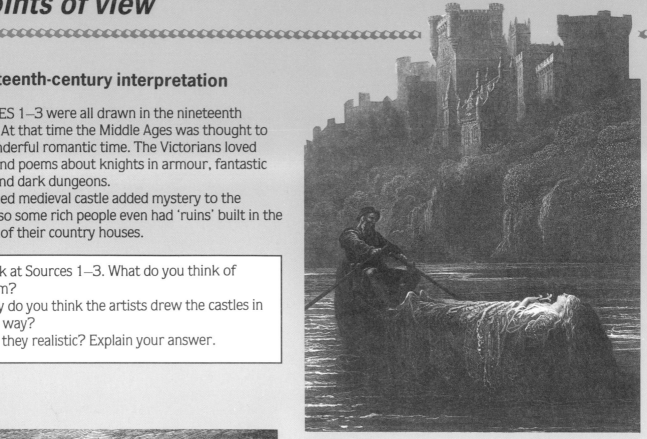

A nineteenth-century interpretation

SOURCES 1–3 were all drawn in the nineteenth century. At that time the Middle Ages was thought to be a wonderful romantic time. The Victorians loved stories and poems about knights in armour, fantastic castles and dark dungeons.

A ruined medieval castle added mystery to the scenery so some rich people even had 'ruins' built in the gardens of their country houses.

1. Look at Sources 1–3. What do you think of them?
2. Why do you think the artists drew the castles in this way?
3. Are they realistic? Explain your answer.

SOURCE 2 Illustration for Alfred Lord Tennyson's poem *Lancelot and Elaine*

SOURCE 1 Nineteenth-century illustration of a castle in Germany

SOURCE 3 Illustration for Tennyson's poem *The Idylls of the King*

A twentieth-century interpretation

Sources 4–6 have been selected to illustrate the story of medieval castles.

SOURCE 4 Harlech Castle, built by Edward I in 1292 to help conquer Wales

SOURCE 5 Beaumaris Castle, Anglesey, the most advanced castle of its time. It was built in 1298 and never captured

▼ **SOURCE 6** Warkworth Castle in Northumberland, built in the early thirteenth century to defend Northumberland against the Scots

1. What impression do Sources 4–6 give of medieval castles?
2. Do you think this is a good selection of photographs to illustrate the story of medieval castles?
3. From the illustrations in this book choose three pictures which you think would be better ones to show the development of castles from the motte and bailey castles of the Normans to the fortified manor houses at the end of the Middle Ages.

Life in the cathedral

SOURCE 1 shows you what you might have seen on a visit to Canterbury Cathedral in the Middle Ages.

It is alive with activity. Every day — not just on Sundays — there are services going on behind the screen in the distance. There are no seats in the NAVE, but townspeople come and go to listen to the services. There are many other churches and chapels in town but the cathedral was built big enough to hold everybody in the town — almost 5000 people. On special feast days they all assemble in the cathedral at nine o'clock and led by the archbishop and clergy they parade around the town.

But today is just an ordinary day and in the background over the hum of the services you might hear the sound of hammering or sawing as workmen — masons, sculptors or carpenters — repair the roof or walls of the cathedral.

A twelfth-century decree said that every cathedral should pay a master to teach the priests and provide free education for 'poor scholars' from the town. A few privileged children of the town are arriving at the cathedral for their lessons, where they are taught by the monks or the priests.

▶ **SOURCE 2** Plan of Canterbury Cathedral

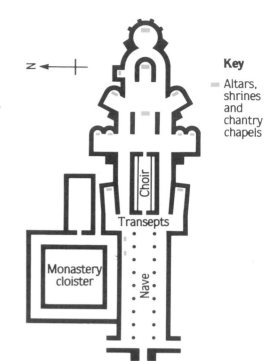

Key

— Altars, shrines and chantry chapels

Choir

Transepts

Monastery cloister

Nave

SOURCE 1 Reconstruction drawing of Canterbury Cathedral

As you can see from Source 2, a cathedral was many churches in one. The CHOIR was the priests' or monks' church. The nave was the townspeople's church. But around the cathedral walls you can see shrines which PILGRIMS came to visit and chantry chapels where special services were said. People believed that one way of improving your chances of getting to Heaven was to pay monks to say masses for you. In Durham, for example, in 1250, the monks were being paid to say 7000 masses per year in cathedral chapels. That works out at eighteen for every day of the year, in addition to the seven daily services they had to run. The wealthiest people could afford to build their own chantry chapel — and to pay their own monk to say services in it.

Canterbury and Durham were monastic cathedrals — attached to a monastery and run by the monks who lived there. But nine of Britain's nineteen cathedrals were SECULAR — run by priests called canons who lived in the town. Life in the secular cathedral could be different.

In Wells Cathedral, for example, traders would set up stalls in the nave, and religious plays were performed there at festival times. In 1300 the plays had become so rude that the DEAN forbade them, and in 1350 he made another edict banning trading in the cathedral.

> **SOURCE 3** Number of chantry chapels in cathedrals during the Middle Ages
>
> York: 36   Exeter: 16
> Lincoln: 36   Chichester: 20
> Wells: 16

1. Use Source 1 and the information above to help you write a short description of a visit to Canterbury Cathedral in the Middle Ages.

> **SOURCE 4** From G.H. Cook's *The English Cathedral through the Centuries*, written in 1957
>
> In the Middle Ages, the naves of some of the secular cathedrals were used by the townsfolk for purposes that would be thought to be in bad taste by churchmen of the twentieth century.
>
> The nave of Old St Paul's was known as 'Paul's Walk' and was the resort of idlers and gossips, a town promenade where people came to rest or walk about. It became the meeting place for rogues and vagabonds, and people played ball within the cathedral itself. Goods were displayed for sale in the nave as in a market hall.
>
> All efforts made by the dean to clear the building of unsuitable behaviour were failures. An act passed by the city fathers in 1554 shows how far St Paul's had sunk: it was forbidden to lead horses or mules or to carry casks of beer or loads of fruit or fish through the cathedral. Doors in the aisles of the nave provided a short cut from the north to the south side of the building.

2. Find two statements of fact and two of opinion in Source 4.
3. Do you think the dean of St Paul's disliked the way his cathedral was used by townsfolk?
4. How did the dean deal with the problem? In what other ways could he have dealt with it?
5. Why do you think the writer of Source 4 disapproves of the way secular cathedrals were used in the Middle Ages?

Pilgrimage

The space beyond the screen shown in Source 1 was normally closed to ordinary people. The only time that they would get to visit the area beyond the screen was when they were on PILGRIMAGE. Since Saxon times English cathedrals had been places of pilgrimage. Pilgrimage was one way that poor and rich alike could ask a saint to help them. At Canterbury there was a fixed ritual for pilgrims. They arrived at the south-west door (see Source 2) and were met by a monk who sprinkled them with holy water. Then the monk led them beyond the screens. They walked on their knees to the tomb and RELICS of St Thomas, prayed to the saint and left gifts.

1. The six windows in Source 5 illustrate a miracle at the tomb of St Thomas Becket. Put the pictures in their correct order by matching them up to the following captions:
   - Richard is taking his horses to graze
   - He sleeps under a tree. When he wakes up he finds he has the dreaded disease leprosy
   - He is back home, but everyone is afraid of catching his illness. Even his mother covers her mouth when she brings him food
   - Richard's parents bring him to Becket's tomb at Canterbury. Richard touches the tomb. A monk gives him a drink of water mixed with Becket's blood. The monk has to take a note of any miracles that happen at the tomb
   - Richard is cured. He is taken to his employer who checks that he is really better
   - The whole family return to the tomb of St Thomas, and give money
2. There is another gift being given at the tomb in the final picture in Source 5. The gifts people gave were supposed to symbolise what they were praying for. Read Source 7, which shows the kind of offerings people gave at saints' SHRINES, and see if you can decide what the other offering in the picture might be.
3. Look at Source 7. What do you think the pilgrims who gave a silver ship, a cart, a wax ear, a walking stick or an iron chain to St Thomas Cantilupe might have been praying for?

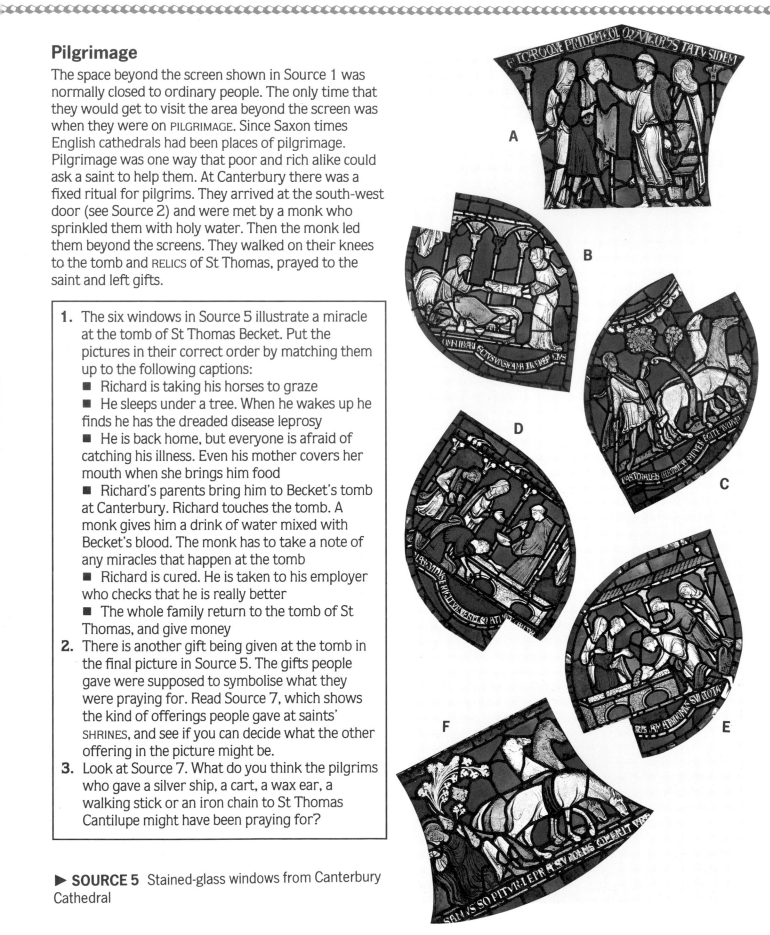

▶ **SOURCE 5** Stained-glass windows from Canterbury Cathedral

SOURCE 6 The relics of St Thomas

4. a) Study Source 6 carefully. What is the story shown on the box?
   b) The box is 17 centimetres wide. What relics of St Thomas do you think might be inside?

SOURCE 7 Offerings at the tomb of St Thomas Cantilupe in Hereford (a different St Thomas from the one in Canterbury)

"
- *170 silver ships*
- *129 silver images, either whole bodies or parts of human bodies*
- *77 figures of horses, animals, birds, etc.*
- *An uncountable number of wax images of eyes, teeth, breasts, ears, etc.*
- *95 silk and linen children's clothes*
- *108 walking sticks for cripples*
- *3 carts*
- *Many belts – men's and women's*
- *Many ladies' jewels, including:*
  450 gold rings
  70 silver rings
- *Iron chains offered by prisoners*
- *Anchors of ships*
- *Swords, spears, lances and knives*
- *An uncountable number of candles* *"*

SOURCE 8 Evidence presented to the Archbishop of Canterbury in 1512 of an attitude that was giving the diocese cause for concern

"The wife of John Baylis went on a pilgrimage to the relics on Relics Sunday (when Thomas' martyrdom was remembered).

When she came home he asked her where she had been and she answered, 'At pilgrimage at the relics, because the parson said that for every visit a man or woman took to the relics she would be pardoned many sins.'

The said John answered, 'He said so because he will have folks' money.'

'No,' she said, 'for the parson said that when the church was burned, the fire had no power over the silk and the relics inside it.'

Then John said, 'When I shall see the relics before me, on the fire, and see that they do not perish, then will I believe them to be holy relics.' *"*

SOURCE 9 Map showing the saints associated with cathedrals and other places of pilgrimage

5. Choose evidence from Sources 5 9 that shows:
   - that pilgrimage was a popular thing in the Middle Ages
   - that pilgrimage was an important source of income for the cathedral
   - that poor and rich people and men and women alike went on pilgrimage.
6. Which is the most useful source for explaining why pilgrimage was popular? Give your reasons.
7. Why might the bishop be worried by the conversation reported to him in Source 8?
8. Look back at Source 8. Using all that you know about pilgrimage and about Canterbury Cathedral, write another ten lines of dialogue between John Baylis and his wife. Begin by thinking how she would reply to John's final comment.

The power of the bishop

SOURCE 10 The bishop's palace and the cathedral in Wells, painted in the fourteenth century

---

1. Which building is the cathedral?
2. Make a list of the similarities between the bishop's palace and a castle.
3. How does the artist show that the bishop is a powerful person?

The bishop had a throne in the cathedral. In fact, the word cathedral comes from the name of the bishop's throne – the *cathedra*. But the bishop might only visit the cathedral for a few days each year. He appointed a DEAN to look after the life of the cathedral for him.

The bishop's real work was elsewhere – out and about in his large DIOCESE, travelling between his various palaces and keeping an eye on the churches under his control. The bishop was the POPE'S representative in the area. Only he could:

■ ordain people (make them into priests)
■ forgive major sins such as murder
■ confirm (accept) new members into the Church
■ settle disputes between people and churches in his diocese.

A bishop also had to make sure that people in his diocese stayed loyal to the beliefs of the Church. Towards the end of the Middle Ages some of the beliefs of the Church came under attack by groups such as the Lollards. So bishops sometimes became involved in trials, such as the one described in Source 11.

SOURCE 11 Extracts from confessions made at the trials conducted by Bishop Langton in Newbury, 1490–1491

I, Thomas Tailour of Newbury, confess that I have called people fools who go on pilgrimage to St James, and have said that there should be more merit in giving a penny to a poor man than in visiting St James.

I, William Carpenter, have said many times that it is not necessary to confess your sins to priests but you can confess them to your fellow men.

I, Richard Lyllyngstone of Castle Combe, confess that whenever there was any preaching from the pulpit I would contradict it at the alehouse.

I, John Tanner of Steventon, confess ... I have preached against baptism.

I, Alice Hignell, confess that when devout Christian people are offering their candles to St Erasmus I have wished I had a hatchet in my hand and were behind them to knock them on the head.

---

4. How did each of the confessions in Source 14 go against what Christians were meant to believe? (You will need to refer to pages 14–17.)

SOURCE 12 All the people who confessed were given similar punishments. This is part of the punishment the bishop gave to Alice Hignell

She is to be led around various towns in the area – when they are at their most busy – bare-headed and bare-legged, carrying a bundle of sticks – a symbol of penance. Her confession is to be read out in public in each place.

Each day for the rest of her life she is to bow before the image of the cross and say the Lord's Prayer five times.

She is not to stray more than two miles from the town of Newbury without the permission of the bishop.

5. Do you think the punishment described in Source 12 is severe?
6. Which of the punishments would it be difficult to enforce?
7. If you had been Bishop Langton would you have dealt with Alice Hignell differently? Explain your answer.
8. Would a bishop have the power to hand out this kind of punishment today?

Visitations

Another of the ways that a bishop controlled his diocese was by going on visitations. The bishop had the right to call all the priests and villagers to give evidence about whether their church was being looked after and whether the priest was doing his job.

SOURCE 13 Visitation report of Bishop Bytton of Exeter to the parish of St Marychurch, Devon in 1301

> *The roof is in bad condition – and the nave and the bell turret have no roof at all.*
>
> *The font has no lock. Most of the books are in good condition, though the gradual [music book] is old and rotten. There is only one surplice, which is in holes. There is no pyx [for holding communion bread] for the Eucharist. The silk for the high altar is fairly good.*
>
> *The parishioners say that until the present vicar's time they used to look after the church. In return they were free from payment of the tithe. Now the vicar makes them pay the tax, keeps it for himself and still expects them to maintain the chancel.*
>
> *Agnes Bonatrix bequeathed five shillings' worth of barley towards the maintenance of the church, but the vicar kept this for himself.*
>
> *The vicar puts his animals in the churchyard and it is made foul. He takes trees in the churchyard which are blown down and uses them for his own building. He prepares his malt [for brewing beer] in the church.*
>
> *The vicar preaches well and carries out his duties in a praiseworthy manner. Often he is absent for a week or a fortnight.*

1. How do you think the bishop got this information? Make a list of the questions his officials may have asked.

2. Do you think the parish of St Marychurch is in a good state?
3. What do the villagers think of the vicar?
4. What excuses do you think the vicar would have for the things the villagers accuse him of?

Activity

After a visitation the bishop then sent an order (called an *acta*) telling the parish what to do about the faults the visitation identified.

Choose three items in the report in Source 13 that you think would most worry the bishop. Write an *acta* to the vicar which will be read to the whole parish explaining what you want them to do and why it is important that they follow your instructions quickly.

How were castles and cathedrals built?

Who did the building?

BUILDING a medieval castle or cathedral was an enormous enterprise, involving many different kinds of workers.

> **SOURCE 1** From the Memoirs of St Edmunds, written in 1094
>
> *Abbot Baldwin orders stone to be brought from the quarries; he calls together stoneworkers; he invites architects; he hires masons and men skilled in the art of sculpture.*

> **SOURCE 2** Written by the builders James of St George and Walter of Winchester in February 1296
>
> *We have masons, stonecutters, quarrymen and minor workmen for making mortar and breaking up the stone for lime; we have carts bringing up this stone to the site and bringing timber. We also have 1000 carpenters, smiths, plasterers and navvies.*

SOURCE 3 A fifteenth-century illustration of a Bible story about the building of the Tower of Babel

1. Use Sources 1–3 to write a list of the different types of workers needed for a large building. For each type of worker you find, write down what work they did.
2. Which of the workers mentioned in Sources 1 and 2 can be seen in the illustration in Source 3? Explain how you worked out what they are doing in the illustration.
3. Source 3 shows an event that probably did not happen. Do you think it is good evidence for building techniques in the fifteenth century?

The master mason

The master mason was the most important person in the building of a castle or cathedral. He was in charge of every stage of the building. Some master masons became so famous that they travelled all round Europe supervising building work. Some were in so much demand that they were in charge of several buildings at the same time. They also became rich. Some owned quarries and made a profit by selling the stone for the new building. Others brought all the workers. They paid the workers' wages and then charged the PATRON a lump sum for their labour.

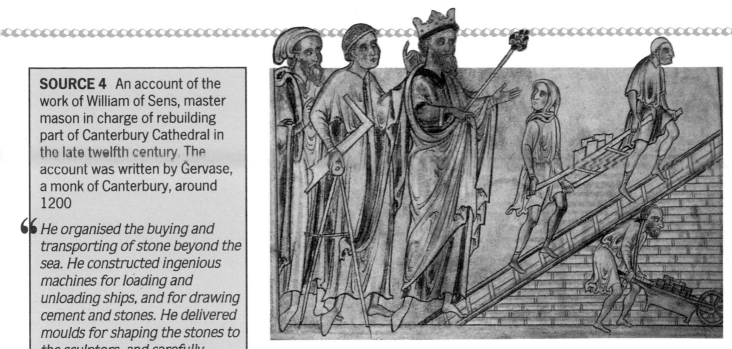

SOURCE 4 An account of the work of William of Sens, master mason in charge of rebuilding part of Canterbury Cathedral in the late twelfth century. The account was written by Gervase, a monk of Canterbury, around 1200

He organised the buying and transporting of stone beyond the sea. He constructed ingenious machines for loading and unloading ships, and for drawing cement and stones. He delivered moulds for shaping the stones to the sculptors, and carefully prepared other things of the same kind.

SOURCE 5 King Offa being shown around a building site by his master mason

4. Look at Source 5. How can you tell which figure is the King and which is the master mason?

The masons' lodge

On every building site there was a masons' lodge (see Source 7 over the page).

At first the masons' lodge was simply a hut where the masons employed by the master mason did their indoor work, stored their tools and ate their dinner. But gradually the lodge also became an organisation of masons. This organisation laid down regulations about the training of masons and standards for masons to keep to. Apprentices were trained for about seven years before they became journeymen. Journeymen could draw up building plans and cut stone into the many different shapes needed. They then practised their craft for several years at a number of different building sites, often far from home, before becoming a mason. The ability to make accurate plans and drawings set masons apart from other workers. Members of the lodge swore to keep the secret of how to draw these plans.

Each mason had his own bench in the lodge. The freemasons all had their own mark since they could not write. This was called their 'bench mark' (see Source 6). They chiselled it onto each block of stone they carved so that it could be checked by the master mason and they could be paid for the amount of work they had done.

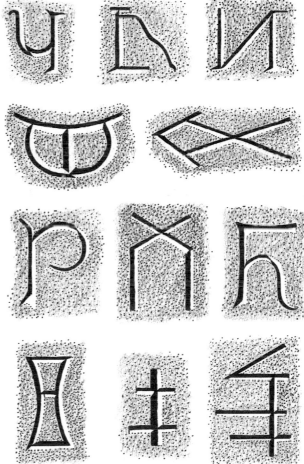

SOURCE 6 Some masons' marks

5. Why do you think masons organised themselves into lodges?

SOURCE 7 Fifteenth-century illustration of a building site

There were several types of mason. The master mason was in charge of the work, laid out the ground plan and checked the foundations. The 'imaginator' carved the decorative statues. The 'setters' were highly skilled and set the tracery and VAULTS which held up the roof. The 'freemasons' carved the blocks of stone for the walls. The 'hardhewers' worked in the quarry. Each type of work was paid according to the skill involved.

SOURCE 8 Records of wages paid in 1495

> *Master masons taking charge of the work and having under them six masons: 7d a day. Freemasons and roughmasons: 6d and 5d a day. Servants of masons: 3d a day.*

Building only took place between February and November. During the winter stone was designed and cut. The normal working day was from sunrise to sunset, with breaks for breakfast, dinner and an afternoon drink.

1. Look at Source 7. Where is the masons' lodge?
2. List all the different jobs being done.
3. What different tools and machines are being used?
4. How are the half-finished walls being protected from the weather?
5. Most drawings we have of masons' lodges show them as open-sided. Why do you think medieval artists showed them like this?

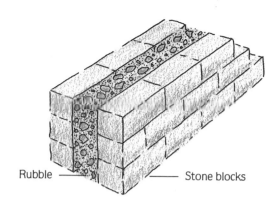

Rubble ——————— Stone blocks

SOURCE 9 Cross-section through a wall

SOURCE 10 Using a template to mark stone ready for cutting

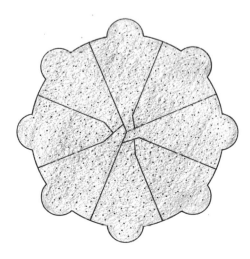

SOURCE 11 Cross-section through a stone pillar

Building techniques

Read this general account of medieval building methods carefully. Then look at the medieval illustrations of building sites over the page. They should give you a good idea of the different stages involved in a big building project and how the problems facing builders were overcome.

First, the ground plan of the building was marked out using poles, ropes, cord and lime. The foundations were dug down to bedrock.

The type of stone used depended on the region, although good stone was sometimes transported over great distances. Norwich Cathedral was partly built of stone from Caen in Normandy. Most castles and cathedrals were built of aslar — high quality blocks of limestone, sandstone, granite or marble — or of rubble, although St Albans Abbey was built of bricks taken from the remains of the nearby Roman city. Rubble was also used to fill in the thickness of the walls between facings of stone blocks (see Source 9). Much of the stone was cut to size at the quarry using the templates of the master mason (see Source 10).

Transport over land was very expensive — the transport often cost more than the stone — so usually quarries were used which were as close as possible to the building site. Water transport was much cheaper and was used where possible. When Rievaulx Abbey was built in Yorkshire, a special canal was built to transport the stone!

The final cutting of stones like those needed for the pillar in Source 11 was done at the site on the ground. The masons did not like doing intricate work on the scaffolding. The stones were lifted in baskets, in wheelbarrows, on shoulders, or by crane or windlass.

The stones were fixed in place with mortar laid with trowels. The mortar used was two parts sand to one part lime. Plumblines were used to make sure the walls were level and straight.

The timber roof of the cathedral was set up before the stone VAULTS were built, for protection against the weather. In winter the tops of unfinished walls were covered in thatch for protection.

The higher the buildings went the more scaffolding was needed, as well as ladders and machines for hauling the stone to the top of a building. There were many types of scaffolding. 'Putlog holes' were left in the wall for the poles holding the scaffolding.

HOW WERE CASTLES AND CATHEDRALS BUILT?

1. Using the information on the previous page, write a description of each of these illustrations, explaining what is happening.
2. Look at the illustrations carefully. What dangers do the workers face?
3. Which gives you the best idea of what building methods were like — the written description on the previous page, or these illustrations?

SOURCE 14

SOURCE 12

▼ **SOURCE 13**

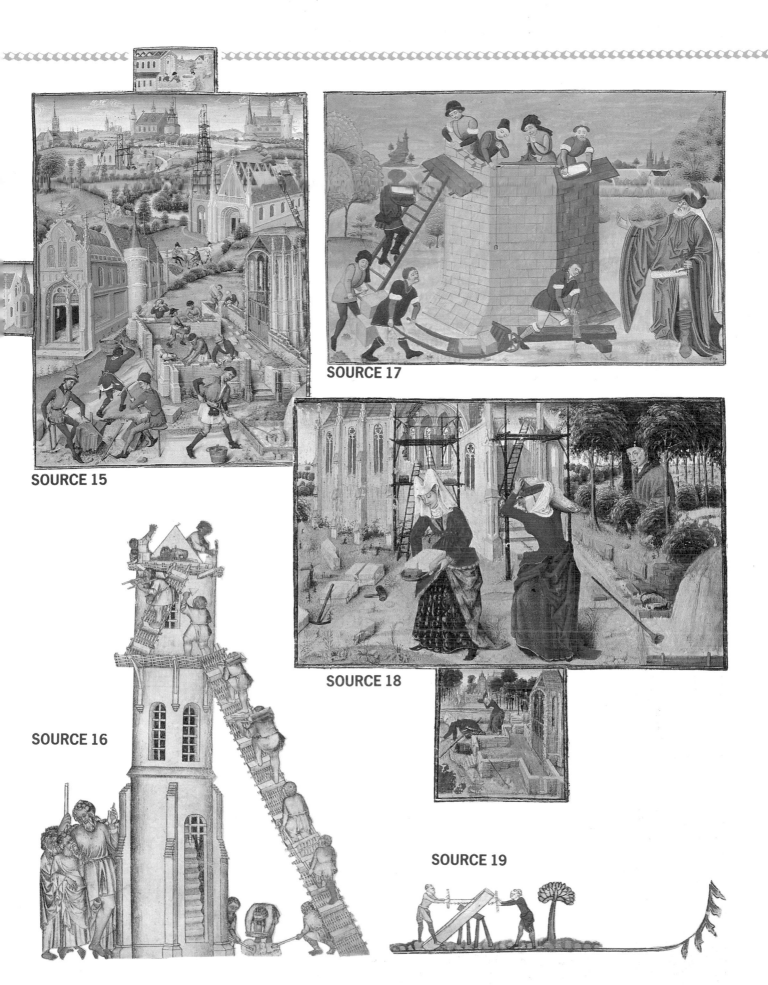

SOURCE 15

SOURCE 16

SOURCE 17

SOURCE 18

SOURCE 19

How was the building work organised?

The king's castles in Wales

At the end of the thirteenth century, Edward I built a chain of massive castles in Wales to deal with the Welsh rebellion. These castles were needed quickly for military reasons and required huge sums of money and an enormous labour force. The King's Works (the department in charge of building for the king) had to find men and materials for this. They pressed (forced) men from all over the country to come to Wales (see Source 20). In 1282, 1000 diggers, 345 carpenters and 50 masons were gathered for just the preliminary work, such as digging the foundations, making the scaffolding and cutting the stone. In 1285, 2500 men were working on the castles. As you can see on the map, Chester and Bristol were the two gathering points for these workers.

The sheriffs of each county were responsible for finding and sending the workers to Wales and for paying them during their journey. Many of these men tried to escape on the journey to Wales and sheriffs often used armed horsemen to guard them. Huge amounts of money were spent – over £93,000 (a vast sum for the Middle Ages) between 1277 and 1339. The workers were paid day wages and were allowed to go home during the winter.

SOURCE 21 The notes of an official in the King's Works. He has written these down to remind himself what to do

Thomas de Normanville to be ordered to provide from his area live oxen, cows and pigs; also from the direction of the northern parts of England; and to send them live to Chester.

Also order him to provide corn in Holderness and elsewhere near the coast and send it to Chester.

The keepers of the diocese of Winchester are ordered to have 1000 quarters of wheat, 600 quarters of oats and 200 quarters of barley carted to Chester.

Remember to seek: 500 carpenters from the counties, to be sent to Chester so that they are there a fortnight after Whitsun. Urgent. Also the maximum number of diggers to be at Chester by the same date. Carpenters and diggers to be forced to work by constables.

Key
- ✒ Diggers
- ⌂ Carpenters
- ✴ Masons
- ▨ 1600 woodcutters
- ⚔ New castles
- ● Gathering points

SOURCE 20 Map showing where workmen came from to build the king's castles in Wales

---

SOURCE 22 Extracts from the building accounts for Harlech Castle, 1286

£15 15s paid to Robert of Walden and 30 others for the hire of 41 carts to bring stone from the quarry.
£10 3s 1d paid to William de Hoxle and 40 others for the hire of 65 horses to bring lime and sand from the sea to the castle.
£40 10s paid to Roger del Wode and 29 others for shipping 405 tons of stone and lime from Caernarfon to Harlech.
10s paid to Robert of Bedford for 100 scaffold poles.
£6 13s 4d paid to Robert the Mason for making a new wall on the sea front with a new tower outside the bailey.
£2 10s paid to carpenters for making the woodwork of the said tower.
15s paid to William the Plumber for roofing the said tower.

Building cathedrals

It usually took much longer to build a cathedral. The master mason would employ a much smaller force of men. Sometimes once the most important part of the cathedral – the CHOIR – was finished the PATRON lost interest and it might be decades before the building was completed. The rebuilding of Exeter Cathedral took 70 years to finish, while the cathedral of Beauvais in France was never finished.

Where did the money come from? When the king had his castles built he raised the money by increasing taxes and by borrowing. Edward I spent so much money on castle building that he was soon in debt. But cathedrals had to be paid for in other ways.

BISHOPS and ABBOTS often built on their own land, or on land that was given to them by a local landowner. These landowners often donated stone and wood from their estates, as well.

Pilgrims gave money when they visited the SHRINES of saints buried in the cathedral. Each cathedral had its own special saint (see Source 9 on page 37). When the choir of St Albans needed rebuilding in 1257 there was a shortage of money. Suddenly the monks discovered the grave of St Alban near the high altar. Pilgrims and money began to pour in.

'Indulgences' were sold to people – in the city of Rouen in France the bishop allowed people to eat butter during Lent in exchange for money.

It was common for people to be ordered by the priest to say prayers to show they were sorry for their sins. Many people paid fines (indulgences) to the priest instead of saying their prayers.

People often left money in their wills for church building. They hoped that this would help them get to Heaven.

SOURCE 23 From the thirteenth-century records of St Albans

66 *Abbot John had been left 100 marks by his predecessor for the rebuilding of the church.*

He assembled the chosen masons, over whom stood Master Hugh Goldcliff (a deceitful and lying man). Before long he had spent the 100 marks and many more. The trench had been dug but the wall did not yet reach the level of its foundations. On Hugh's advice carvings were added that were inappropriate and far too expensive. Before half the work rose to the height of one storey, the abbot began to grow weary of the whole thing and the work stopped. The wall lay uncovered in the winter weather, the stones being fragile broke into bits and the wall collapsed. The workmen left in despair and their wages were not paid to them.

The abbot now appointed Brother Gilbert to be in charge of the work. The abbot paid for the work by contributing one sheaf from every acre of sown land. The work continued slowly. The abbot was keen to see the work completed in his lifetime and so he gave many gifts of gold and silver to advance the work. He sent a clerk around the diocese with relics of saints. He collected a lot of money. But the work absorbed all the money and still little progress was made.

The years passed by, Brother Gilbert died, and the work passed to another brother who added two feet to the walls in 30 years. 99

Changes in cathedral design

Just as castle design changed during the Middle Ages, so cathedral design changed as well. Builders began to build taller, more decorated cathedrals with more windows and thinner pillars. It is sometimes possible to work out how old a cathedral is just by looking at its design.

Study Sources 24 and 25. One of the cathedrals was built between 1090 and 1140. The other was built between 1220 and 1258.

Look at the lists below, which point out some of the differences between the styles of cathedral building in 1090 and 1220. From the information given decide which of the two cathedrals is Norman and which is Gothic or Early English.

1090: Norman

- Round arches
- Thick walls
- Small windows
- Huge thick pillars
- Flat wooden roofs
- Short square towers
- Not much light inside the cathedral

1220: Early English/Gothic

- Pointed arches
- Thinner walls
- Tall windows
- Thinner pillars
- Stone roofs
- Tall towers with spires
- A lot of light inside the cathedral

1. Which cathedral looks the most beautiful to you?
2. Which looks the strongest?

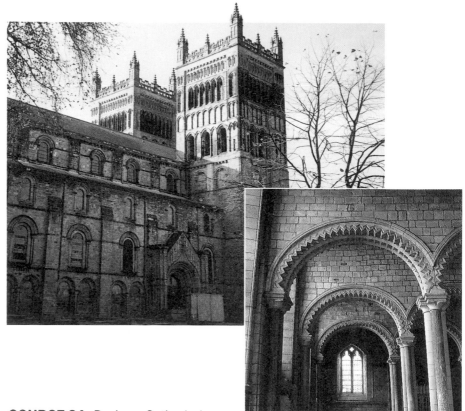

SOURCE 24 Durham Cathedral

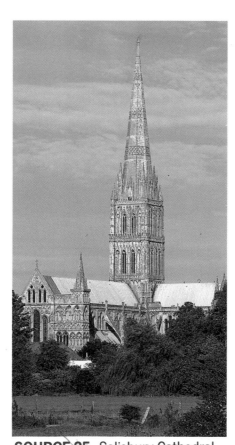

SOURCE 25 Salisbury Cathedral

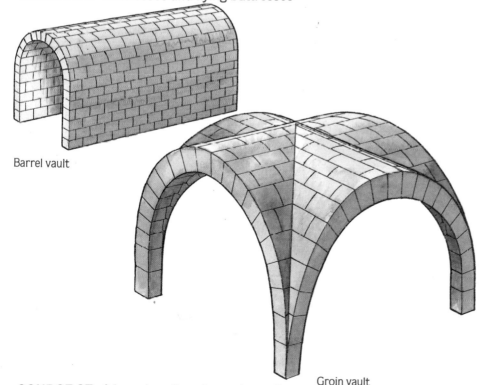

Roof

Vaulting

Weight of roof pushes walls outwards

Weight of buttresses pushes in opposite direction

Wall buttress

Flying buttress

SOURCE 26 Buttresses and flying buttresses

Barrel vault

Groin vault

SOURCE 27 A barrel vault and a groin vault

Keeping the roof up

Many English cathedrals, especially the Gothic ones, are enormous, yet they look very fragile. Not only are the walls often full of huge windows, but above the walls are heavy stone VAULTS and lead roofs. How is all this weight kept up? Why doesn't the building collapse?

All the weight bearing down has to be absorbed somehow. The master masons solved this by building buttresses (see Source 26). If the cathedral had aisles 'flying buttresses' were needed so that the weight was taken out over the aisle to the buttresses on the outside. The master masons had to work out how much buttressing was needed — too little and the building would fall down. In 1284 Beauvais Cathedral collapsed because of this.

The weight of the roof was distributed to the buttresses by the ceiling vaults. As the Middle Ages went on different types of vaults were developed. Look at the two in Source 27.

The barrel vault spread all the weight evenly along the whole wall. This meant large windows could not be built into the walls because the walls would be too weak to hold the vault up. Now look at the groin vault. Here the weight is concentrated at four points. These could be reinforced, while the walls could have large windows built into them.

> **1.** Draw a labelled diagram explaining why the groin vault was better than the barrel vault.

A brand new cathedral

Once a medieval cathedral was built it might be improved and repaired in later years. But occasionally a cathedral might be knocked down and built again from scratch. Sources 28–31 show the imaginary story of the building of a brand new cathedral in France. The building work took more than 100 years.

> 1. Put the pictures in the correct order.
> 2. Write a caption for each picture.

▶ SOURCE 29

SOURCE 28

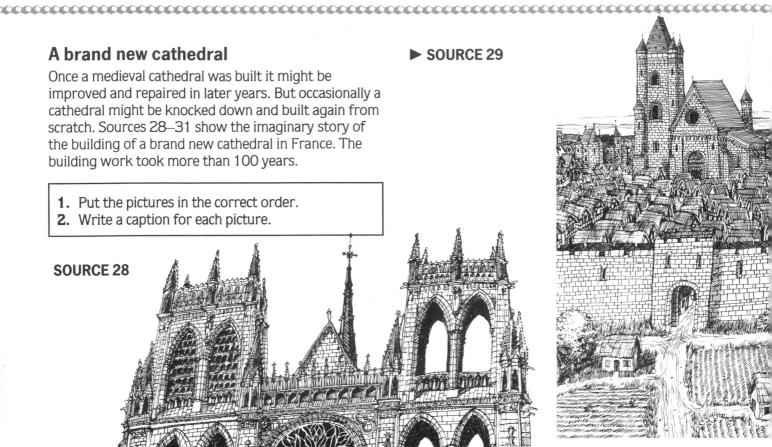

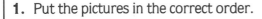

SOURCE 30

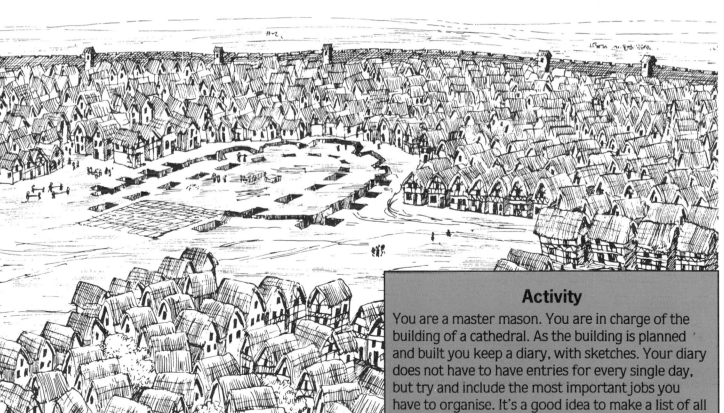

Activity

You are a master mason. You are in charge of the building of a cathedral. As the building is planned and built you keep a diary, with sketches. Your diary does not have to have entries for every single day, but try and include the most important jobs you have to organise. It's a good idea to make a list of all these jobs first.

Investigating a castle and a cathedral

A site visit to Lewes Castle

RECENTLY a party from a Sussex school went on a site visit to Lewes Castle in Sussex. As part of their preparation they had studied the castle guidebook, which included the picture in Source 1.

As the pupils went around the barbican (the gatehouse) at the castle they had to decide whether Source 1 was an accurate picture or not.

SOURCE 1 A nineteenth-century drawing of the barbican, from the Lewes Castle guidebook

SOURCE 2 Photograph of the machicolations of the barbican, taken on a recent site visit

1. Study Sources 2–4. What do you think? Is Source 1 accurate? Give as many reasons as possible for your answer.

SOURCE 3 Reconstruction drawing of the gatehouse of Lewes Castle

SOURCE 4 Information from the castle guidebook

The castle is built on chalk [which absorbs water].

2. Say whether you agree or disagree with this statement: 'Source 1 must be inaccurate because it is different from the castle as it is today.'
3. Suggest how an inaccurate picture of the castle might have come into existence.
4. The figures in the drawing are wearing costume from the middle of the nineteenth century. Can this source tell us anything about how people in the nineteenth century viewed Lewes Castle?
5. Make a list of ways a site visit can help you find out more about a castle or cathedral.

A site visit to Rochester Castle and Cathedral

In the next few pages we take you on a 'site visit' round Rochester Castle and Cathedral. On the site visit you will be able to use the understanding you have gained from this unit about:

■ why castles were built and why they changed
■ what life was like in cathedrals and castles in the Middle Ages
■ how castles and cathedrals were built.

You will look closely at the buildings and practise some of the skills of detailed observation, recording and detective work that make a site visit worthwhile. You will also see how documentary evidence can help us understand the history of castles and cathedrals.

1. Look at Source 5 and identify: the cathedral, the KEEP, the CURTAIN WALL (round the BAILEY), the bridge over the river Medway, and the town centre of Rochester.
2. Why do you think the castle is in a worse state of repair than the cathedral?
3. Get into groups. Study Source 5 carefully. Make two lists:
   ■ a list of things you can find out about Rochester Castle and Cathedral from Source 5 alone
   ■ a list of things you'd like to know about Rochester Castle and Cathedral that you can't tell from Source 5.

SOURCE 5 Aerial view of Rochester Castle and Cathedral as they are today

Investigating Rochester Cathedral

Outside the cathedral

LOOK at Source 1. The cathedral is not one building but several, built at different times and joined together in a complicated arrangement. Sources 2–5 show you what you can see at various points as you walk around the cathedral at Rochester.

> **1.** On your own copy of Source 1 mark where each of the photos in Sources 2–5 were taken.

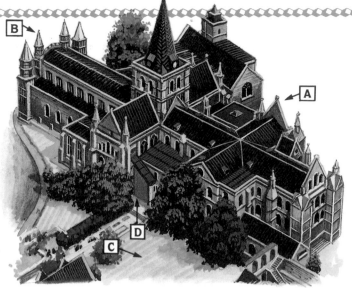

SOURCE 1 Rochester Cathedral as it is today

> **5.** Look at Source 3. This has been the main entrance of the cathedral since the Middle Ages. How did the builders try to impress medieval visitors?
>
> **6.** Make a field sketch to show the shape of the West Front. Label the features you have listed in your answer to question 5.

SOURCE 2 Gundulf's Tower. This tower is the oldest part of the cathedral building. It was built in 1078 by the first Norman bishop, Gundulf, who was famous for building castles as well as cathedrals and monasteries

> **2.** Make a field sketch of Gundulf's Tower. Label it to show how it is different from the rest of the cathedral. For example, compare the walls and windows in the rest of the cathedral with what you can see in Source 2. (Look at Source 9 on page 63 to see how much detail to put on a field sketch.)
>
> **3.** Can you think of any reasons why this tower is different from the rest of the cathedral?
>
> **4.** A cathedral was built at Rochester in 670, long before Gundulf's time. What do you think might have happened to the old buildings?

SOURCE 3 The West Front and the great entrance, built about 1150

SOURCE 4 The south side, rebuilt around 1300. This is well away from the main entrance of the cathedral

7. Look at Source 4. What is the feature labelled A called?
8. It was added long after the wall was built. Why do you think this was?
9. Why do you think this side of the cathedral was not decorated like the West Front was?

► **SOURCE 5** The ruined cloister, part of the monastery where the monks who used to run Rochester Cathedral lived. The monastery became a ruin after it was closed down by the king in 1540

10. What clues in Source 5 suggest that these buildings might once have been important?

Look back at Source 5 on page 53. You can see that the cathedral is right in the middle of the town. In the Middle Ages it was an important part of town life.

SOURCE 6 Medieval rules regarding the Medway bridge

"The cathedral had to look after part of the bridge over the Medway. In return, the cathedral received a quarter of all toll payments, and for the two days of the feast of St Andrew all toll payments."

SOURCE 7 From a medieval agreement between the bishop and the monastery

"I, Gundulf, reserve to me from the estates of the monastery, every year at the feast of St Andrew:
■ sixteen hogs cured for bacon
■ 200 fowls
■ 1000 lampreys [eels]
■ 1000 eggs
■ four salmon.
If I shall be absent from the feast then the provisions be distributed to the strangers and poor."

11. Read Sources 6 and 7. In what ways was the cathedral important in the life of Rochester? Explain your answer.

Inside the cathedral

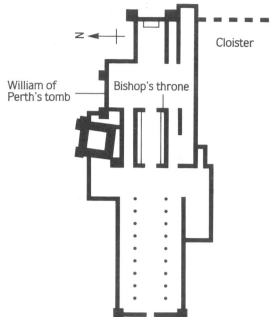

SOURCE 8 A plan of Rochester Cathedral

SOURCE 9 The high altar, where the monks took religious services. Ordinary people did not see this part of the cathedral

1. Make a copy of the plan in Source 8 and label the NAVE, the CHOIR, the north and south TRANSEPTS, Gundulf's Tower and the West Front.
2. Mark on your plan where the photos in Sources 9 and 10 were taken from.

SOURCE 10 Part of the north wall of the nave

3. Look at Source 9. What clues are there that it shows a very important part of the cathedral?
4. Why do you think ordinary people were not normally allowed to go to the altar?
5. Look at Source 10. Which features have been added since the Middle Ages?
6. Make a labelled field sketch of Source 10.
7. With a partner, think of reasons for the differences between the arches and reasons for the half-finished arch. Write down your ideas.

SOURCE 11 The crypt – a mysterious cellar underneath the altar. The monks might use it for praying. Religious services also took place here. The bones of Saint Paulinus are buried somewhere beneath the stones of the crypt floor

SOURCE 12 Faces at Rochester Cathedral

> **8.** Why do you think the roof of the crypt is shaped like it is?
> **9.** How would the crypt have been lit in medieval times? Do you think it would have been very light or very warm?

> **10.** People have suggested that the faces in Source 12 may be portraits of the people who built the cathedral, or that they might be designed to scare off devils and evil spirits. What do you think is most likely?
> **11.** Why do you think many of the pictures can no longer be seen on the cathedral walls?

Saint Paulinus is not the only saint buried at Rochester. In 1201 a Scottish pilgrim bound for the Holy Land, William of Perth, was murdered near Rochester and buried in the cathedral. Very soon miracles were reported at his tomb. He was made a saint. Pilgrims flocked to Rochester, and gifts poured into cathedral funds. This may have been one reason why the monks were able to start rebuilding the arches in the nave (see Source 10).

When you visit a cathedral always remember to look up at the roof as well as down at the ground. All around the cathedral, above some of the doorways and at the ends of arches, are carved faces like those in Source 12.

There are also several places where the faded remains of paintings and drawings can be seen on the cathedral walls. It seems likely that at one time the cathedral was a much more colourful place, covered with bright pictures. These were not just there for decoration. The pictures usually had a religious message and were used to teach people about Christianity.

Activity

Opposite the bishop's throne in Rochester Cathedral there is a tiny fragment of a medieval wall painting called the 'Wheel of Fortune'. Many of the wall paintings were in the nave, where everyone could see them. This one was in the choir, where it would only be seen by the bishop and the monks.

1. The Wheel of Fortune was a common picture in the Middle Ages. Read this description of a Wheel of Fortune and then draw your own version of the picture: 'God, or Jesus, is sitting on a throne using a handle to turn an enormous cartwheel. Six figures are shown clinging to the wheel. They are meant to be the same person at different stages in his life. At the beginning he is a child. At the top of the wheel he becomes a king. But as the wheel turns he falls off and at the bottom he is a penniless beggar.'
2. What message do you think this picture is supposed to give to the bishop and the monks?

The great pulpitum divide

ROCHESTER Cathedral was once part of a Benedictine monastery, most of whose buildings have now disappeared. In the Middle Ages, the people of Rochester shared their cathedral with the monks who lived in the monastery. The monks sang the services in the CHOIR behind the screen (see Source 8 on the previous page), which in the Middle Ages was called a *pulpitum*. The townspeople listened from the NAVE.

SOURCE 2 The pulpitum

The demands

> **SOURCE 1** Written by a nineteenth-century historian
>
> 66 *There is no cathedral in England where the choir is more completely cut off from the rest of the church than Rochester.* 99

A	Put a statue of the Virgin Mary in the nave

B	The townspeople should raise money for a bigger and more glorious pulpitum

C	The pulpitum should be removed so that the townspeople can see and hear the services better

The pulpitum became a symbol of the division between the monks and the town — which sometimes developed into squabbles over who should control the cathedral. You are going to play a game which will help you to understand the squabbles between monks and townspeople.

A meeting has been called to try to sort out the problems. Both sides will be making several demands at the meeting. You have to decide which demands each side is going to make.

D	The townspeople should buy a new library of religious books for the monks

E	The townspeople must stop bringing animals across the cathedral grounds

Get into groups of six. Half of each group will be monks, half will be townspeople.

F	The monks should say free masses for the souls of the sick and dying

Aims: monks

You live a very quiet and ordered life. Your whole day is organised according to strict monastery rules. For you the cathedral is a special place where you have devoted your whole life to worshipping God. The townspeople are often noisy in the cathedral during the services and they do not really understand your way of life.

You do not want to ban them from the cathedral because you want them to learn about God, and you need the money they bring to the cathedral. Your main aim is to keep some parts of the cathedral private, and to preserve the way of life your monastery has followed for centuries.

Aims: townspeople

The monks run the cathedral but you feel that they are trying to keep it too much to themselves, and that they ought to do more for ordinary people. Since your own parish church, St Nicholas, was knocked down, you have been given a special townspeople's altar in the cathedral nave. But you want to be able to see what goes on in the choir and near the high altar.

Your ancestors helped to build the cathedral, and the wealthy townspeople still give a lot of money to keep it running. You think that you should have more influence over what is done with that money and what happens in your cathedral.

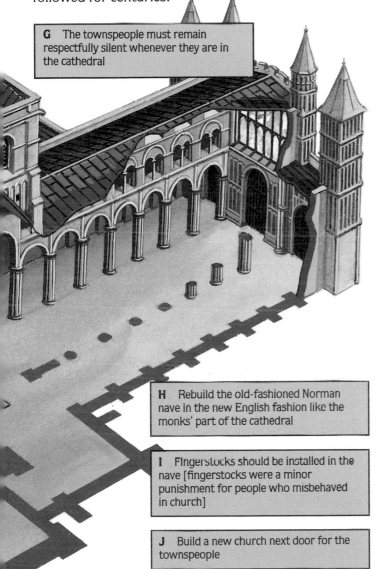

G The townspeople must remain respectfully silent whenever they are in the cathedral

H Rebuild the old-fashioned Norman nave in the new English fashion like the monks' part of the cathedral

I Fingerstocks should be installed in the nave [fingerstocks were a minor punishment for people who misbehaved in church]

J Build a new church next door for the townspeople

K The townspeople must stay out of the cathedral except at service times

L The monks should spend more time teaching the townspeople to read and write

---

How to win

1. Look through the demands which either side might make, which are shown opposite.
2. Reread the aims of your group if necessary.
3. Discuss with your partners which demands *your* side is going to make. Choose the most important four.
4. Put these four into order of importance. What would be the order of importance for your side in the Middle Ages? Think carefully about the order you put them in as this could win or lose you the game. When it comes to scoring time you will find that the demands people in the Middle Ages would have put high are worth more points to you than the ones they would have put low down.
5. When you have agreed an order of importance write the letters of the demands down in that order.
6. When all groups have completed their lists pass yours to your opponents and your teacher will tell you how to score.

---

1. Your teacher will tell you the order of importance that the writers of this book put the demands in. Do you agree with their order?
2. Write a letter to the POPE from the townspeople or the monks putting your case to him, explaining why you are making these demands and asking him to help you.
3. Which of these demands – if any – do you think were met in real life? Ask your teacher.

Investigating Rochester Castle

Outside the castle

IT is only a few paces from Rochester Cathedral's door to the CURTAIN WALL of the castle. In the early days after the Norman Conquest the owner of the castle – William's half-brother, Odo – tried to take over land belonging to the cathedral. Ten years later the new Bishop Gundulf got King William to settle the dispute between the castle and the cathedral. Gundulf himself later built the curtain wall around the castle.

The curtain wall (Source 1) was built in 1080 – 50 years before the KEEP (see Source 3). With only the curtain wall to defend it the castle withstood a long siege in 1086, as described in Source 2.

SOURCE 3 The keep today. The smaller tower in front is called the forebuilding

The curtain wall has been constantly rebuilt and improved since 1086 with new towers, such as the one built by King Edward in 1337 (Source 4).

SOURCE 1 Part of the curtain wall today

SOURCE 2 Ordericus Vitalis describes life in the castle during the siege

Countless flies were bred in the excrement of men and horses. They were nourished both by the heat of the summer and by the breath of so many people closely pent up. Swarms of flies horribly infested their eyes and noses, their food and drink. They could not eat their meals either by day or night, unless a great number of men were employed in turns to flap the flies away from the faces of their comrades.

---

1. What other measures could the besieged soldiers have taken to deal with the problems described in Source 2?

SOURCE 4 King Edward's Tower today

2. Look at Sources 1, 3 and 4. Look back at Source 5 on page 53 and work out where these photos were taken from.

3. Explain how towers such as the one in Source 4 made the curtain wall easier to defend.

4. Estimate how tall the towers of the keep are. To help you, the door on the forebuilding (see Source 3) is two metres tall.

5. Make a field sketch of the keep. The keep not only looked impressive and showed how powerful the lord was but also had features that made it very difficult to attack. Mark on your sketch five features that you think made the keep difficult to attack.

6. How would you explain the holes in the walls of the keep marked A, B and C?

7. The entrance to the keep is inside the forebuilding near the top of the ramp. Some of the entrance defence is now missing. Add to your field sketch a drawing of what you think is missing. (Clue: look at Source 5.)

8. Look at Source 5, which shows what the castle might have looked like in the Middle Ages. Using the evidence on this page, do you think this is a drawing of the castle in 1100, 1250 or 1400?

9. Look at Source 1. What evidence is there in that picture that would have helped in making the reconstruction drawing in Source 5?

10. What other evidence do you think the artist could have used?

11. Compare Source 5 with Source 5 on page 53. What differences are there?

Activity

Write a paragraph of description for a new guidebook to Rochester telling people what they would see as they walked from the west entrance of the cathedral to the entrance of the castle keep.

SOURCE 5 A reconstruction drawing of the castle

Inside the keep

SOURCE 6 A cross-section through Rochester Castle keep

SOURCE 7 The inside of the keep from ground level. The walls are three metres thick

1. For living purposes the keep is rather like a medieval version of a block of flats. Make a list of problems which the inhabitants of the keep might have faced in the Middle Ages.

SOURCE 8 The second level of the keep

Look at Source 8. Although the floor is missing you can see the rows of square holes in the stonework (A) where wooden beams would have held up the floorboards.

In the foreground is the central wall (B). This was built to make the whole keep stronger, but it also helped to divide up the keep into different rooms.

The chapel was also on this second level and there were garderobes (toilets) and passageways in the thickness of the walls.

2. Match up the features labelled C–D on Source 8 with the following descriptions:
   ■ Well shaft
   ■ Fireplace.
3. Do you think this is the level of the keep that the lord lived on? Explain your answer by referring to the evidence on this page.
4. Even this level would have been quite cold and dark by modern standards. Look back at Source 1 on page 20 to remind yourself of what a keep might look like inside. Do you think the lord would say his keep was comfortable to live in? Would he think comfort was important?
5. Compare Source 8 above with Source 5 on page 55. Make a list of similarities and differences. Do you think there is any evidence that parts of the keep and parts of the cathedral were built around the same period?

The mystery of the round tower

Look at Source 9. Compare the towers of the keep. Can you think of any reasons for the difference between them? You may have some good theories. We will look at other evidence to see if they are right.

SOURCE 9 A recent field sketch of Rochester Castle keep

Source 10 comes from the Barnwell Chronicle, which was written by a monk. It tells us that in 1215 the castle was owned by King John. William de Albini, with 100 knights, rebelled against the King's rule and took over the castle, so John had to fight to get it back. In 1215 the King laid siege to the castle. Source 10 tells us what happened after several weeks of siege.

SOURCE 10 From the Barnwell Chronicle

John put expert miners to work. They cut their way underground until at last they were under one of the great corner towers. They put wooden beams in to hold up the roof above their heads. After two months, when the miners came out, brushwood and branches were carried into the tunnels and fat from forty pigs. Then a fire was started. All the timbers caught fire and blazed until they collapsed. With a great roar the castle walls cracked and the whole tower fell down. But the defenders did not surrender until they had nothing but horseflesh and water to sustain them.

---

1. Why do you think John's soldiers needed pigs' fat?
2. Draw a diagram to show what happened to the tower.

The King recaptured the castle and had the tower rebuilt. But why did the builders make the new tower a round one, and not square like the other towers?

Round towers were certainly the latest fashion. Look back at page 26 and see if you can find reasons why round towers might have become fashionable.

---

3. Why do you think the King rebuilt the tower as a round one, not a square one?
4. Look at Source 11. Have the builders tried to blend in the new tower with the older stonework?
5. Why do you think the King allowed such messy work in the keep?

SOURCE 11 The wall inside the keep where the new tower was joined to the original keep

continued ▶

Conclusion

Now that you have found out about Rochester Castle and Cathedral look at Source 12.

SOURCE 12 A modern mural of Rochester Castle used on the cover of the Rochester Visitors' Guide, 1990

1. Compare Source 12 with the evidence on pages 60–63. Do you think Source 12 is accurate? Explain your answer.
2. What details in it are most accurate?
3. Now look back at your definitions of a castle and a cathedral from page 4. Is there anything about them that you would like to change after studying this unit?

Glossary

abbot the head monk in a monastery (abbey)
Anglo-Saxons people from Germany who ruled England from the fifth century until 1066
archbishop a chief bishop, in charge of all the bishops, priests and people in a large area of the country

bailey the flat outer part of a castle, with a ditch and a fence or wall around it
baron a powerful lord who was granted land by the king
bishop a man responsible for running the religious life of a **diocese**, based at the cathedral of the diocese
buttress a large stone support built up against a wall. A **flying buttress** is only joined to the wall at the top

Celtic people who lived in Britain before the Romans took over
choir the part of a church or cathedral east of the **transepts**, where the choir sings
concentric castle a castle with two or more rings of walls, one inside the other. The inner walls were usually higher so that archers could shoot from both walls
crenellations the battlements along the top of a wall
Crusades holy wars to conquer the Holy Land, declared by Christians during the Middle Ages
curtain wall a wall that runs around the **bailey** of a castle

dean the priest responsible for the running of a cathedral
diocese the area of the country for which a bishop is responsible. Medieval dioceses covered hundreds of square miles

keep a fortified tower in a castle where most of the people lived

mine a tunnel dug under the corner of a castle **keep** to make it collapse
motte the mound, often artificial, on which a castle **keep** is built

nave the main area of a church or cathedral, where the people stand for services

patron a person who ordered and paid for a castle or cathedral to be built
pilgrimage a journey to a holy place such as a **shrine**. People who make a pilgrimage are called pilgrims
Pope head of the Roman Catholic Church

relics part of a dead holy person's body or belongings, usually thought to have the power of working miracles

secular priests or a church not part of a monastery
shrine a place sacred to a holy person, often a tomb

transepts in a cross-plan cathedral, the transepts are the arms of the cross, usually separating the **nave** from the **choir**

vault an arched roof or ceiling
villein a peasant who was under control of the lord of the manor in the Middle Ages